od and Mad

TRANSFORM ANGER
USING MIND, BODY, SOUL AND HUMOR

Jane Middelton-Moz, M.S., Lisa Tener, M.S., Peaco Todd, M.A.

Cartoons by Peaco Todd

Health Communications, Inc.
Deerfield Beach, Florida

www.bcibooks.com

Library of Congress Cataloging-in-Publication Data

Middelton-Moz, Jane, date.
    Good and mad : transform anger using mind, body, soul, and humor / Jane Middelton, Moz, Lisa Tener, Pesco Todd ; cartoons by Peaco Todd.
        p. cm.
    Includes bibliographical references.
    ISBN 0-7573-0102-9
    1. Anger.   I. Tener, Lisa   II. Todd, Peaco.   III. Title

    BF575.A5M519 2003
    152.4'7—dc21

                                                                        2003051091

Publisher: Health Communications, Inc.
            3201 S.W. 15th Street
            Deerfield Beach, Florida 33442-8190

Cover illustration by Peaco Todd
Cover design by Peter Quintal
Inside book design by Lawna Patterson Oldfield
All cartoons by Peaco Todd ©2003

This book is dedicated to the peacemakers:
those who pray for peace and then put feet on their prayers.

CONTENTS

Acknowledgments xv

How to Use This Book xix

    Exploring the Nature of Anger xx

    Getting the Most from This Book xxiv

CHAPTER 1

WE ARE FAMILY: The Roots of Anger 1

    Childhood Beliefs About Anger 1

    The Unfair Odds of Self-Hate 5

    Learned Helplessness 13

    Anger All Around Us 17

    Anger-obics[SM]: Move Your Body, Shift Your Mind 22

        Yo' Goals • Hopscotch • It's a Mad, Mad, Mad, Mad Word • Popeye Meets Deepak

    Mad Pad 25

CHAPTER 2

LIGHT MY FIRE: Sparks That Incite Anger

LIGHT MY FIRE: Sparks That Incite Anger 27
When Your Buttons Get Pushed..28
Core Issues and Triggers 36
Overlooking Your Needs and Boundaries 39
*Anger-obics*SM: Move Your Body, Shift Your Mind............................44
   Gratitude Attitude • Whoa, Trigger • Whoa, Trigger II • Emotion in Motion • Think Thank
Mad Pad 54

CHAPTER 3

BAD COMPANY: Unhealthy Anger

BAD COMPANY: Unhealthy Anger..57
Confronting Unhealthy Anger Styles..57
Depression, Addiction, Compulsion and Illness..................................65
Passive Aggression 72
The Rages...73
*Anger-obics*SM: Move Your Body, Shift Your Mind............................77
   This Guy's the Limit • Walk on It • The Golden Healing Light • Home Sweet Home
Mad Pad 81

CHAPTER 4

BRIDGE OVER TROUBLED WATER: Feeling Vulnerable................................83

The Blame Game 83

Fear of Failure 88

Making Assumptions About Others 89

*Anger-obics*ˢᴹ: Move Your Body, Shift Your Mind..................................95

    Solar Power • Solar Power II • Humor Me • Duck Back • Safety Plan

Mad Pad 101

CHAPTER 5

LET'S GET PHYSICAL: Anger in Your Body....................................103

Anger as a Physical Experience 103

When You're Hungry, Lonely, Sick or Tired 107

Consumption, Chemistry and Body Cycles 110

How Unhealthy Anger Affects Your Body 112

*Anger-obics*ˢᴹ: Move Your Body, Shift Your Mind................................117

    Body Language • Salome's Silky Scarf Dance • Map the Pain • Clay-by-Clay

Mad Pad 122

CHAPTER 6

GETTING TO KNOW YOU: Anger and Couples

GETTING TO KNOW YOU: Anger and Couples...125

The Peaks and Valleys of Intimacy 125

Acknowledging the Patterns of the Past 128

Cultivating a Vibrant Relationship 131

Handling Conflict in Healthy Ways..135

Anger-obics^{SM}: Move Your Body, Shift Your Mind........................141

    Changing the Game • Stop 'til You Drop • Domino Effect • Bye Low, Cell Hi!

Mad Pad 147

CHAPTER 7

HUSH LITTLE BABY: Anger with Our Children

HUSH LITTLE BABY: Anger with Our Children 149

Separating Your Past from Your Children's Present 149

Recognizing Children's Developmental Stages...153

Strategies and Techniques 154

Your Child and Bullying 164

Anger-obics^{SM}: Move Your Body, Shift Your Mind........................167

    Sounds Right! • Lighten Up • Animal Crackers • Masquerade

Mad Pad 171

CHAPTER 8

WE CAN WORK IT OUT: Conscious Conflict 173

The Nature of Healthy Conflict 173

Establishing Ground Rules 176

Tools for Mastering Conflict..179

Reaching Closure 184

*Anger-obics*ˢᴹ: Move Your Body, Shift Your Mind....................................187

    Choosy Mothers Choose • Sherlock Holmes

    • What's So Funny About Peace, Love and Understanding? • Part-toons

Mad Pad 191

CHAPTER 9

I CAN SEE CLEARLY NOW: Healthy Anger...193

Anger as Motivation for Making a Difference 193

The Healing Power of Humor 195

Anger and Creativity...198

Anger and Grief 199

Creating New Patterns: A Step-By-Step Process 201

Creating Peaceful Communities 206

*Anger-obics*ˢᴹ: Move Your Body, Shift Your Mind....................................214

    Role Models • Walk to the Beat • Passion in Action • Blast from the Past • Picasso-rama

Mad Pad 222

CHAPTER 10

THE BEAT GOES ON: The Practice of Forgiveness 225

The What and Why of Forgiveness 226

Taking Responsibility for Your Own Experience 230

Practicing Forgiveness 235

When You Need to Forgive Yourself 241

Anger-obics^{SM}: Move Your Body, Shift Your Mind 245

    Let Freedom Ring • Hula Hips • Poem Blessing • Yoga Mudra

Mad Pad 249

CHAPTER 11

TAKE ME TO THE RIVER: Anger, Spirituality and Purpose 251

When You're Angry at God or the Universe 251

Incorporating Anger Work into a Spiritual Practice 256

Anger and the Power of Purpose 261

Anger-obics^{SM}: Move Your Body, Shift Your Mind 264

    Soul Talk • Spiritual Warrior • Cell-a-Brate • Circle of Friends

Mad Pad 269

Appendix A: Conscious Conflict Quick Guide..271

Appendix B: Conscious Conflict: An Example 273

Appendix C: Sample Scenarios (for use in *Anger-obics*SM exercises)............275

References and Resources 277

ACKNOWLEDGMENTS

The authors thank Frances Brisbane for her compassion, beauty, friendship and continual belief in the human spirit. Without her this book would not have been possible.

The authors thank Lisa Drucker for her expert knowledge and editorial support, and the continued support and caring of Peter Vegso, Susan Tobias, Larissa Henoch, Terry Burke, Kim Weiss, Kelly Maragni and the whole staff of Health Communications.

We thank Clare Sartori Stein for her wise input into the exercises. Thanks to those who provided or inspired exercises: Alaya Chikly, Jeff McFarland and Tricia Newport Hart. Thanks to all who tested the *Anger-obics*^{SM} exercises and read parts of the manuscript, in particular: Octavia Porter Randolph, Gerri Davis, Chris Ellis, Tracy Sukraw, Taylor Ellis, Tricia Armstrong, Brenda Beauregard, Susan Moreland, Linda Jackim, Pat O'Brien, Patty Shepherd, Lindsa Vallee, Brian Chmielewski, Jonathan Powell, Shawn Crawford, Gene Joy, Christina Gombar, Val Kilmer, Charlotte McLean, Nancy Gray, Seraina McCarty, Tracy Hart, and Diane and Bill Laut. We offer a special thanks to John Bradley, Esq., for giving us his legal advice and assistance.

A special acknowledgment to the beautiful, creative and courageous elders, adults and youth we have met in our travels, as they continue to teach us of the depth and strength of the human spirit.

Jane would like to acknowledge the heart gifts, wisdom and endless support of her loving family: Her children, Shawn, Jason, Damien, Lisa, and Forrest Lesch Middelton, Melinda and Michael Knight, Suzy Goodleaf, Diane Labelle and Sarah Healy for their endless support and love; her beautiful grandchildren, Logan, Canaan, Anastasia Middelton, Christopher and Ryan Flannery, and Jamie and Sage Labelle Goodleaf for the gifts of their love, laughter, wisdom and patience as grandma took time to write this book; her brother and sister-in-law Alex and Marina Ward for their loving support; and to her extended family—Rod Jeffries for his support, compassion, love and humor; and Luke, Sam, Jean and John Jeffries for their love and support. Thank you all for being the wonderful people you are.

Jane also would like to thank Roger Strauss and the staff of the Institute of Professional Practice for their time, energy, kindness and laughter, and for being the wonderfully supportive people they are; and Diane Laut for her competence, beauty, laughter and never-ending personal support.

Jane would like to give a special thank-you to the friendship, support and love of Elaine Lussier, Wanda Gabrial and Paul Ferland, Vera Manuel, Mary Lee and Denny Zawadski, Christine and Stan Grof, Ann and Terry Harrmann, G. Johnson, Bill Laut, Denise David, Annie and Don Popert, Lizzie E. Saunders and Charlie M. Gordon, Alex Smith and Gina Delmastro, Harold and Joy Belmont, Mary and Ken Carter, Shirley Walker and Jean Jacque Guyot, Annie Alaku, Tammy and Emile Picard, Mabel Louie, Jackie Thomas and the compassionate staff with whom she has worked at Carrier-Sekani Family Services, Margaret Antoine and the Healing of Healers Group, Mary Aitchison and the courageous people with whom she has worked in Nunavik, Quebec.

Lisa thanks her family for their love, support and contributions to the book: Her husband Tom, for his love and editorial support; her son William, for sharing his mom; her parents, Marty and Elizabeth Tener; Diana and Joey Arnold; Alan and June Tener; her mother-in-law, Mimi Sammis—for so much, but especially the lessons she has taught her about peace and positive thinking, Sam and Jinny Sammis for their hospitality in Vermont and for all the love and support they've given her family; Anne, Bob, Nell, Jack and Mia Patterson-Potter, Lee Patterson, Annabel Patterson, Hedy Schneider, Anne and Howard Nissman, and Jane and Herb Herschlag.

Lisa thanks her professional and spiritual communities: the International Women's Writers Guild (IWWG) and Hannelore Hahn; writer's circle; board, volunteers and staff of Hospitality Homes in Boston; UUCSC; Women's Lodge, Katherine's circle, and Wednesday morning dancers. Thanks to those who provided sage advice and encouragement along the way—Rita Rosenkranz, Virginia Swain Baratta, Ann Marie Healy, Rosalind Michahelles, Cindy Kottas. Thanks to her wonderful friends and baby-sitters for their support and love.

Lisa lovingly appreciates the teachers and healers in her life: Angelica and Carlos Cubides, Doug Janssen, Chris and Katherine Carbone, Martha Schwope, Steffi Shapiro, Martine Rini, Fred Stalman, Rong Zhang, Lili Cai, Dr. John Han, Barbara Ganim, Judy Krulewitz, Cynthia Wood, Pam Geib, Bill Ryan, Eileen Murphy, Oliver Wilson, Patty Shepard, Ann Drake, Carin Roberge, John O'Brien, Christian Brunner, Marilyn Bishop, Mary Stracensky and Joan Cremin.

Peaco wishes to thank her incomparable Success Team—Olivia Miller, Kathe Gregory, Maggie McNally, and Daryl Juran—for their wisdom and friendship. She would like to thank her friends and colleagues in the National Cartoonists Society who show her every day what a powerful art form cartoons can be. She thanks Marc Abrahams of *The Annals of Improbable Research* for his friendship and professional guidance. She is grateful to her wonderful students in Lesley University's Learning Community Bachelor's program for their intelligence and courage, and for hanging in there with her.

Peaco offers heartfelt gratitude for the love of her "adopted" mother, Nee Picket, and her "adopted family":

Naila Beg; her beautiful goddaughter, Leila Fettig; and Zaccur, Rabi and Earle Fettig. A very special thanks to Chris Cooke, Ph.D., who offered such invaluable guidance at the beginning. To those incomparable writers she is privileged to know as both friends and exemplars: Marnie Mueller, Susan Quinn, Alice Hoffman, William Least Heat-Moon, and the inimitable Amy Tan. For their years of sustaining encouragement she thanks her friends: Katrin Achelis, Jaci Barton, Vern Grabel, Barbara Porro, Ruth Belmeur, Lyn Raney, Bob Nesson, Ellen Kramer, Andrea Wolf, David Cohen, Joyce Caras, David Holzman, Arleen Sherman, Frank Trocco, Hank Gross, Shankar Sastry, Linda Jue, Peter Plamondon, John Wyatt, Christie Baxter, Pilates goddesses Lisa Silveira and Martha Mason, and so many others who bless her life with their presence.

She thanks her wonderful family: all the Todds and Gilmores for the love and acceptance they've offered over the years. Finally, she feels incredibly fortunate to be married to John Bradley, in her eyes the sweetest, funniest, smartest and most supportive husband on the planet.

Jane, Lisa and Peaco are grateful to each other: for what their collaboration has taught them about anger, integrity and humor, and for making the journey all the more amazing.

EXPLORING THE NATURE OF ANGER

Experiencing and communicating your anger in healthy ways can be the key to greater personal strength and integrity, increased intimacy and deeper fulfillment. If you have the tools that enable you to recognize, understand and express your anger in positive ways, you might discover that anger actually enriches your life. *Good and Mad* was created to give you those tools.

Talking about anger can be confusing because the word can mean many things. "Anger" is used to refer to both the raw emotion and its accompanying physical sensations, and it also is used to refer to the response to that emotion. When we focus on the anger that is a response, we realize we can respond in both positive and negative ways, ways that are healthy or unhealthy.

Since many of us experience unhealthy anger *as* anger, it's no wonder that it feels like such a problem. However, *healthy* anger can act as a powerful force for positive changes in our lives at every level. While unhealthy anger can be harmful to ourselves and others, healthy anger can be a gift that opens up communication and allows for connection between people.

Same Old Song

Tanya's best friend at work is laid off while the manager's nephew, who rarely works, is promoted. Tanya's furious, but she's afraid to act or speak out for fear of losing her job. When she gets home she sees that her husband Mark has left his breakfast dishes in the sink and his gym clothes on the bedroom floor. "That selfish jerk," she mutters as she begins to pace around the room.

Mark is barely through the door when Tanya launches into a tirade. "Who do you think I am, the maid?" she shouts. "You *always* do this to me!" Tanya's harangue takes Mark by surprise—he didn't use that many dishes, and he doesn't see what the big deal is. He's tempted to yell back but instead decides to stonewall. "You know I had an early meeting this morning. Leave me alone!" He walks into the bedroom and slams the door. Minutes later, he reappears still wearing his work clothes. "I refuse to talk to you when you're being unreasonable," he says in a steely voice. "I had a hard day and thought I could depend on you for a little TLC. But I guess I was wrong. I'm going out so don't bother to wait up."

Later that evening, after she has washed the dishes in a fury (in the process breaking her favorite mug) and gulped a glass of wine, Tanya begins to feel ashamed of her tantrum. She wonders if her outburst had something to do with her frustration with work and her fear that there's nothing she can do about the situation. She knows that she overreacted to Mark's mess even though "who cleans up" has been an ongoing issue between them. She resents his leaving and not talking things out.

When Tanya was a child, her parents would argue and then subject each other to the silent treatment, occasionally for days—Tanya hated those times, and she hates thinking that her marriage might be continuing that pattern. Boiling with confused emotions, she flings herself on the bed and starts to cry. When Mark returns later, he finds Tanya asleep. He covers her with a quilt and crawls into bed, feeling a miserable mixture of shame and defiance. By morning they've both decided not to bring up what happened, hoping that it will simply go away. Things gradually return to normal, until the next time some seemingly minor incident sets one or the other off.

What *Is* It About Anger?

More than any other emotion, anger can be difficult to understand and hard to endure. As Tanya and Mark demonstrate, anger is a complicated feeling often involving other emotions, physical sensations, patterns learned as a child and triggers from the past. Our anger may also be linked to behavioral patterns such as blaming someone else for our situation, or deciding that we're powerless to affect our circumstances or to change what hurts or displeases us.

Often anger is our immediate reaction to a situation that is disturbing or distressing. Anger can be a clue that something needs to change, that something is wrong. These simple descriptions, however, don't address the complexity of the experience or the ambivalence we may feel when trying to deal with angry feelings.

One of the most confusing characteristics of anger is that sometimes we don't even recognize when we're feeling angry. Many of us are so uncomfortable with feeling anger that we deny it altogether. Anger, especially anger that is denied, can hide behind other feelings and behaviors, such as resentment, criticism, overeating or depression. Only when we erupt into sudden fury, perhaps triggered by some seemingly trivial incident, do we realize that we're angry. Even then, we may not understand why and instead hit on the most superficial, least threatening reason, leaving the deeper causes of our anger unexamined.

Fears about anger are not necessarily unfounded. Expressing anger can involve taking an emotional risk. Letting someone know you're angry can feel like you're starting something that might escalate in uncontrollable and unpredictable ways. You may worry that expressing your anger could cost you a valued friend or colleague. You're not alone if you find anger (yours and others) the hardest emotion to accept or express.

Some people are reluctant to look at anger. They have felt hurt or seen other people hurt by various expressions of unhealthy anger: rage, violence, sarcasm or put-downs. They have learned to associate anger with trouble, and conclude that anger is best left unexamined and unspoken. However, the old adage "least said, soonest mended" offers only temporary peace: Unresolved anger is not likely to disappear.

GETTING THE MOST FROM THIS BOOK

Because anger can be complex and daunting, *Good and Mad* offers a multidimensional approach to transforming your experience of anger. By engaging mind, body, creativity, spirituality and humor, *Good and Mad* provides an array of tools to help you access anger's power to positively change your life.

People access information in a variety of ways and on many levels, and *Good and Mad* is designed to appeal to many different learning styles. The features of this book include:

- Informational text, designed to give you a framework for understanding the nature and causes of anger, and to help you develop skills for dealing with anger and expressing healthy anger
- Our own innovative *Anger-obics*ᔆᴹ exercises, intended to engage your body, mind, creativity and spirit as you discover new ways to approach your experience of anger
- *Mad Pad* journal pages, which include thought-provoking quotations to accompany your journey and inspire your reflections—you'll find both lined pages for writing and unlined pages for drawing or writing
- A series of cartoons, featuring a diverse group of characters who deal with angry situations in humorous and insightful ways

Whatever your learning style—whether you think of yourself as a visual (sight-oriented), conceptual (mind-oriented), kinesthetic (body-oriented), aural (listening-oriented) or experiential (project-oriented) learner, or some combination of all those styles—you are sure to find that *Good and Mad* offers an approach to understanding and transforming your anger that will work for you.

How to Use the Anger-obics℠ Exercises

As you work on the *Anger-obics*℠ exercises, here are some points to keep in mind:

Transformation and Change Happen in Stages

The first step toward change is the desire to change, the willingness to give up behaviors that aren't working. Then comes understanding. Many of the exercises, particular early ones, are designed to help you understand your anger. They help you recognize beliefs or patterns of behavior. Once you understand your actions and their effects, it's easier to change. Sometimes understanding where the anger came from makes it easier to leave the ghosts of the past behind and create change in the present.

The second group of exercises focuses on shifting or transforming your anger. You can work on these exercises alone or with the person with whom you are angry. The third group of exercises focuses on the heart of the battle: What to do when you are angry, in the moment. Some exercises combine two or more of the three objectives.

The Exercises Are Designed to Tap Into Different Learning Styles

We now know that some people learn best when they are moving their bodies—tapping, molding clay, taking notes or rubbing their chins. These people have a kinesthetic learning style: They need to touch, feel or move in order to learn. Some people are more visual and need to see things. If that describes you, pictures, images and color probably enhance your learning. Others need to hear things or say things to learn best. Some people like to dance; others like to meditate.

The *Anger-obics*℠ exercises are designed for people with many different learning styles. What that might mean for you is that some exercises are going to feel great. They will tap into your strengths and make sense. Other exercises may be more difficult. Try to stick with these if you can. Sometimes a real breakthrough can happen when you are stretching yourself with a less comfortable style. On the other hand, it's fine to skip exercises. If you find yourself thinking, "I must not have done this right because it just didn't work," remember that people learn in different ways and adjust your thinking to, "Not all the exercises are going to work for me."

You may find yourself wanting to employ an *Anger-obics*^{SM} exercise while you're away from home—at work, at a friend's house or visiting your in-laws. Consider writing your favorites on index cards and carrying them in your purse or wallet. *Anger-obics*^{SM} can be at your fingertips in seconds!

At the end of each set of *Anger-obics*^{SM} exercises you'll find two journal pages we're calling the *Mad Pad*. The first page is lined and intended for you to write on. The second is unlined and can be used for drawing, writing or whatever you like. In some of the chapters, we suggest that you further explore a particular point by writing about it on your *Mad Pad*. You may also use these pages to record insights, reactions to the *Anger-obics*^{SM} exercises, responses to the quotes, or in any other way you wish. Since space within the book is limited, you may wish to supplement the *Mad Pad* pages with your own notebook for journaling, drawing, etc.

Get Help if You Need It

Some people find that after a particularly powerful exercise, they stop working on the exercises altogether. Here are some suggestions if that happens to you:

- You may need time to integrate any strong feelings that come up.
- You can return to the Gratitude Attitude or Golden Healing Light meditation for clarity and calm. These *Anger-obics*^{SM} exercises are at the end of chapters 2 and 3, respectively.
- It may be prudent to contact a therapist to get help with particularly intense feelings or issues that come up.

There may be times when you need strategies fast—you're in the heat of anger and don't have time to go back to the book. Prepare for these moments throughout your reading. When you read about strategies you think might be helpful, list them on a *Mad Pad* page or in your journal notebook. You may even want to copy the list and post it somewhere handy.

A Note About Language

Anger is a feeling: Like any emotion, it's neither positive nor negative—how we experience and respond to anger is what makes it healthy or unhealthy. Throughout this book, we make a strong distinction between healthy and unhealthy anger. However, for the sake of easier reading and a smoother flow, sometimes we use the term "anger" to mean either healthy or unhealthy anger; which one we mean should be clear from the context.

Healthy anger can be a blessing in your life. Learning how to express healthy anger is a skill worth working toward—it will improve your communication with others, help you to better meet your own needs, and enable you to feel more connected and closer to the people you care about. Healthy anger has the power to reveal your deep and wise self, and guide you toward becoming a person who acts in the world with purpose and compassion.

A Note About the Vignettes

The individuals and situations mentioned in the vignettes are composites of many people and locales. The impact of unhealthy anger on individuals and communities is frequently similar. Any similarity of these examples to specific individuals or communities is only a result of these common characteristics.

CHAPTER 1

WE ARE FAMILY:
The Roots of Anger

Most of our beliefs about anger, and our responses to this complex emotion, develop when we are young. This chapter explores how beliefs and patterns can originate in childhood and the ways that these beliefs and patterns affect us now. We look at how shame and helplessness from the past can influence your present relationship with anger. We offer you ways to begin changing negative thinking. We help you begin to develop new strategies to support healthier behaviors and a more fulfilling life.

CHILDHOOD BELIEFS ABOUT ANGER

Susan and Jake were newlyweds. In their first few weeks of married life, they were delighted to discover that they shared many of the same habits, including reading at night before falling asleep. One night, after several weeks of marriage, they were comfortably settled in bed reading and blissfully unaware that the first fight of their married life was soon to erupt.

Jake had had an exhausting day and read only for a short time. He yawned, put his book on the bedside table, kissed Susan and turned out the light on his side of the bed. Susan was not tired and continued reading.

1

Soon, Jake began tossing and turning. Susan looked up from her reading and asked Jake if her light was bothering him. She said that if it was, she would be happy to read in the other room. "No dear, that's all right," Jake responded. Yet, his words did not match his behavior. He continued to sigh loudly at regular intervals, and his tossing and turning became more dramatic, often shaking the bed. Susan asked several more times if Jake would like her to turn her light off. Finally, having had enough, she screamed, "Just answer me, DO YOU WANT THE LIGHT OFF OR NOT!" Jake was silent. Susan bolted from the bed yelling, "That does it! If you can't be honest with me about something as simple as wanting a light off, how can I possibly trust you? I obviously don't know you at all!" Susan spent the night on the couch. She slept little, waiting for Jake to come after her and apologize. By dawn she was entertaining fantasies of leaving him. For his part, Jake slept soundly through the night.

The following day Susan spoke with a wise friend who pointed out that there might be "ghosts" hanging around their bedroom: Susan and Jake's childhood experiences and beliefs about anger. He helped Susan realize that she and Jake needed to understand the past in order to change the present.

Before We Are Six or Seven or Eight

Most of what we learn about conflict resolution and anger expression comes from our families of origin. Jake grew up in a family where anger was never expressed directly. If his mother was angry, pots and pans would bang and crash in the kitchen. This kitchen calamity would be followed by loud silences. If his father was "displeased," he would become emotionally distant, and would smile and become unpleasantly pleasant if spoken to. Jake was careful never to have an opinion about anything for fear of upsetting someone and suffering the emotional abandonment that followed.

Susan grew up in a "war zone." She said that living in her family was like living with one emotional bomb in the basement, another in the attic, and never knowing when one of them might go off. She learned to be hypervigilant at all times, reading cues, calming the "angry beasts" or removing herself from the situation. She needed to know what people were feeling at all times in order to protect herself. She hated silence the most because explosions were always preceded by heavy silences.

It is not surprising that Jake and Susan's bedroom was "haunted." Neither realized that their anger expression, and the ways in which they dealt with disagreements, were dictated by ghosts from the past. Both had firmly promised themselves that they would never behave like their parents.

Where Oh Where Is "Just Right"?

Many of us grew up in families where the expression of anger was:

- "Too hot," emotionally or physically violent
- "Too cold," distancing and abandoning
- "Too hard," judging, righteous and blaming
- Or "too soft," with few limits or boundaries, few guidelines or little accountability for behavior

Both Jake and Susan feared conflict and anger and had no idea what normal was. Avoidance of normal, healthy anger and conflict often creates the unhealthy anger we learned to fear, which reenforces our avoidance, and the beat goes on.

By age five, many children have already learned that anger is not acceptable. They learn this through observation, punishment, shaming, or having love and affection withdrawn. What were the lessons your parents, grandparents, uncles, aunts, siblings and other family members taught you about anger and conflict? What do you tell yourself when feeling angry or faced with conflict?

Know the Myths You Learned

Below are some common myths about anger and conflict. Are you surprised that some of them are myths? Which of the myths did you learn? How do these myths affect your expression of healthy anger today? You may wish to make note of them on your *Mad Pad*—the pages at the end of this chapter (after the *Anger-obics*^{SM} exercises), designed for journaling and other notes.

- If I state an opinion, I will create conflict.
- Anger is about winners and losers.
- If I get angry, I will be abandoned.
- Anger is violence.
- If you want a good marriage or friendship, avoid anger and conflict.
- The biggest or loudest always wins an argument.
- If I feel angry, I am a bad person.
- If I feel angry, you have to do things my way.

Are there others you would add to the list?

Healthy Attitudes About Anger and Conflict

The following are some facts about expressing anger and resolving conflict. You may want to make note of the ones that surprise you on your *Mad Pad*. (You can come back to these statements when you finish the book and see if you agree.) Which facts, if any, did you learn in your childhood? How has this knowledge affected your expression of anger and your willingness to resolve conflicts?

- Conflict is normal. There are healthy, productive and kind ways to engage in conflict.
- Letting others know when we feel angry can build trust.
- If we never express our opinions, we cannot build trust. Expressing our opinions is essential in building trust.
- Healthy conflict builds intimacy by helping us work out together the issues that matter to us.
- Healthy expression of anger is part of healthy communication.
- Everyone is entitled to his or her feelings. The feelings of others belong to them, not us. (Because another is angry does not mean that we have to take on his or her battles or change who we are or what we do.)

Are there others you would add to the list?

THE UNFAIR ODDS OF SELF-HATE

For some people, buried shame is one of the taproots of anger. In such cases, it is important to uncover, understand and begin to heal the shame in order to address the anger. As self-esteem increases, it becomes easier to deal with feeling angry in a healthy manner.

Shame is a deep-seated feeling of not being worthy. When shamed, we feel overwhelmed, self-conscious, exposed, visible and examined unfavorably by a critical other. Shame is the feeling that the "examination" has found us unworthy and imperfect in every way. We hang our heads, stoop our shoulders and curve inward, wanting desperately to be invisible. We begin to lack self-confidence, have poor self-esteem and suffer from endless internal judgment. Shame is self-hate, and self-hate is the inclination to blame ourselves for everything that happens, to see ourselves as deficient and deserving of mistreatment (Middelton-Moz, 1990).

Self-hate can be defined as the sense that, "No matter what I do, I can't change the reality that who I am in the core of my being is unacceptable." Developing self-hate is a long process. Children take from the outside, and bring to the inside, beliefs about who they are at the core of their being. The way they're touched or not touched, looked at, talked to, disciplined, given attention or ignored, determines who they believe themselves to be. Many children have gazed at a cracked and distorted self-image most of their lives. The most beautiful child can believe herself to be ugly if that is what is reflected back to her. A child, left in a crib to cry, can develop self-loathing in the earliest days of life. A child who is punished for crying or expressing normal anger can learn that tears and anger are unacceptable, and will limit emotional expression in order to be acceptable. A child who seeks out nurturing and instead is abused will learn to feel ashamed of both his body and his normal, healthy, developing sexuality.

Children who can never quite live up to the expectations of others may believe they are not capable, develop chronic procrastination, or stop trying. Children who have been bullied continually in school may learn to see themselves as worthless, powerless victims and may continue to surround themselves with people who emotionally and/or physically abuse them.

We may learn that vulnerability, culture, ethnicity, appearance or even the way we move is unacceptable. We engage in self-hate when we hate any aspect of ourselves. We may feel anything from mild discomfort to complete disgust or revulsion for part or all of our being. We may learn to hide our real self and develop an ideal self instead. That ideal self may be someone who never cries, never gets angry, is tough and macho, must be perfect and never make a mistake, must work to the point of exhaustion, or must attempt to hide his culture or ethnicity behind an "acceptable" mask. The process of self-hate takes on a life of its own as we reach adulthood, injuring and depleting all that is real about us.

People who are shamed continually subject themselves, as they were once subjected, to an internal tyrant who rarely sleeps and who acts as judge, jury and executioner of the spirit. This inner oppressor judges aspects of the self as bad and in need of punishment if allowed to surface. The shameful parts of the person might include, but are not limited to, anger, tears, vulnerability, mistakes, fear, helplessness, race, ethnicity, looks, intelligence or beliefs. Many people have learned through shaming experiences that to make a mistake is to *be* a mistake.

When we feel shame, we feel that we are failures, defective and unworthy of love. Shame's constant companion is fear of abandonment. We develop a derivative sense of self: "You're nobody until somebody loves you," and become hypersensitive to perceived attacks and criticism from others. Once a threat is detected, a loud internal warning signal sounds, and an individual may immediately fight to salvage a fragile sense of self by blaming, criticizing, flying into a rage or otherwise further shaming him/herself. When we feel shame, we also feel rage that is directed inward towards an already fragile self or outward to unsuspecting others. When we grow up being shamed by our parents, teachers, relatives or other children we learn multiple responses: to shame ourselves as we once were; to surround ourselves with others in our lives who continually put us down; or to shame, blame and attack others in the same way we were blamed, shamed or attacked.

The following are shame messages that you may tell yourself, hear from coworkers or loved ones in your life, or may give to others in your life—your friends, partners, children, etc. Feel free to add to the list. After the list is complete, check off the messages you give yourself; the messages you frequently receive from friends, relatives, coworkers or partners; and the messages you give others.

Messages	Receive from Others	Give Self	Give Others	Constructive Counter-Messages
"You don't belong here."				
"How many times do I have to tell you?"				
"You're such a crybaby."				
"You always make a big deal out of nothing."				
"You're too fat."				
"What kind of a person are you anyway?"				
"If he/she only knew, you wouldn't be loved."				
"You shouldn't bother anyone."				
"What you think isn't important."				
"You never do enough."				
"You're unlovable when you act like that."				
"Can't you do anything right?"				
"You're not worthy of such attention."				
"Who do you think you are anyway?"				

Messages	Receive from Others	Give Self	Give Others	Constructive Counter-Messages
"Why can't you be more like _____?"				
"You're only lovable when you _____."				
"You really fooled them."				
"You're such a wimp."				
"You're stupid."				
"You're such a fake."				
"You're always _____."				
"You'll never amount to anything."				
"You're so needy."				
"They'll find out you're _____, then they'll leave."				
"You're always in the way."				
• _____				
• _____				
• _____				

Now, try to identify where the messages you give yourself, allow others to give you or give others, came from originally (parents, extended family, teachers, siblings, peers, neighbors, etc.) What can you do the next time you begin to shame yourself, others shame you or you feel like shaming someone else? Try to counter the shaming message with something constructive, such as:

- Interrupt it with another message: "My needs are important, too!"
- Set limits: "I want to know how you're feeling, but it is not okay to put me down."
- Learn other ways to express frustration, hurt or anger that are not emotionally hurtful to another: "I need to sort out my feelings by myself right now."

When we grow up with "distorted mirrors," we develop a distorted image of ourselves. It is important to find people in our lives who can be "honest mirrors" and can help us heal from shame. They can support us by lovingly reflecting back who we really are, not the distortion we may have learned.

LEARNED HELPLESSNESS

It was a day like many others in the life of Sandra Jones: up at barely five o'clock; start the coffee; quick shower; wake, dress and feed the baby; wake Tommy and James and tell them the bus will be there soon; wake and hold her screaming toddler who does not like being awakened, then dress and feed her; wake her husband, Bill, who decidedly isn't a "morning person"; shout at Tommy and James, threatening mayhem, destruction, withdrawal of privileges and any number of failures in life if they don't, in fact, "get moving!"; kiss the air next to her husband who is now leaving for work; load her ill-tempered children into her ancient car only to find the battery dead again; call a neighbor for a jumpstart; drop Tommy and James off at school and the little ones at day care; and finally speed to her own job, yelling at "thoughtless" drivers along the way.

Sandra's only break of the day was filled with phone calls: the bank whose recent balance did not match hers, thus the bounced check; the electrician who had promised to install her new dishwasher; the trash collector who had missed the delivery. Unfortunately, the bank's computers were down, so she couldn't straighten out the mistake on her last statement. For what seemed like the hundredth time she could reach only the electrician's answering machine. The waste-management company said that "according to their computer" her garbage had, in fact, been picked up.

At two o'clock, Sandra received a call from the school that James had sprained his ankle on the playground. Taking the time off work that she could ill afford, she drove at breakneck speed to the emergency room where she held her crying child while attempting to answer questions regarding her insurance and signing papers assuring that she would pay the bill. She then waited with her son for two hours, frantically trying to soothe James then running to the pay phone to tell her husband to pick up the other children.

Later that night after much screaming at the children to "go to sleep," tripping countless times over the new dishwasher that wasn't installed, listening to Bill's curses at bills that he was attempting to pay with too little money, she and Bill had what had become their nightly fight about who did more and how unappreciated each felt, blaming each other for the problems in their marriage. At last, in complete frustration, Sandra began throwing things at Bill, mostly objects he had carelessly left around the house rather than put away. "Living with you is like having another child," she screamed as she hurled his shoes that had been in the middle of the floor at him. For his part, Bill again threatened that he wasn't sure how much more he could take, as he proclaimed that Sandra was "not the easygoing, fun-loving woman" he had once loved.

Learned helplessness is a major factor in marital conflict, rage and depression. It is the sense that you have little control over your environment and the actions you take on your own behalf don't seem to make a difference. Sandra and Bill, like millions of people today, are trying to parent, work at their jobs and handle the stresses of day-to-day living with too little time, energy and support. The job of raising a family at one time was shared by extended family—Sandra's lack of extended support and her stress in dealing with computers and answering machines compound her feelings of helplessness and frustration.

Many people tell us that their lives feel out of their own control. One man we encountered actually kicked a bank machine. When he realized he had been seen he replied, "I know I just made a fool of myself, but it doesn't seem to matter what I do anymore. Computers are in control. Have you ever tried to talk to a computerized voice? What I do doesn't seem to make a difference."

Runaway technology, lack of support, feelings of isolation, increased psychological stress, financial pressure, and a perceived chasm between rule-makers and the people they govern can, at least in part, account for increasing symptoms of unhealthy anger in our society. What is certain is that the link between anger, depression and learned helplessness—and the increase in all three—is becoming more obvious.

Once Sandra and Bill began to understand that their unhappiness was a result of their circumstances rather than their love and commitment to each other, they began to find ways, within their means, of reconnecting. Sandra arranged to trade baby-sitting duties with another mother so that she and Bill could rejoin the bowling league where they had met. Bill checked into his company's tuition-reimbursement program and discovered that they would pay for him to complete his accounting degree. He entered school and is looking forward to the time when his new degree will earn him a promotion and a raise.

Sandra and Bill also decided to allot an hour after dinner one night a week, with no TV, to enjoy quiet time as a family and share what's going on in each other's lives. While they have not solved all their problems or eliminated feelings of helplessness from their lives, they are beginning to feel more in control. The "downtime" that they've programmed into their schedule makes it easier to handle the stressful times without completely "losing it."

Can you think of ways in your own life that you can decrease feelings of helplessness and feel more in control? Can you get more support? Are there ways you can feel more connected to others? Are there people in your life you have allowed to command power over you? You may want to answer these questions on your *Mad Pad*. Make a list of pressure-releasers and ways to relax more. All these can help you exert, and feel, more power over your circumstances.

Everybody's Talkin' at Me—Nobody Hears a Word I'm Sayin'

Here is a list of situations that often trigger a sense of helplessness in people:

- Being stuck in traffic
- Computer going down
- A telemarketer calling

- Reaching an automated "menu" system when phoning for help or information
- All the children needing things at once
- The baby crying incessantly
- Being forced to take time off from work because of needs at home even though you need the money
- Being confronted by a hostile service provider
- Being told that the computer is right and you are wrong
- Everything pulling on you at once (your partner, your children, work, etc.)
- Having a parking place taken by another driver when you only have ten minutes to pick up something at the grocery store

On your *Mad Pad* write about the items from the preceding list that make you feel helpless, and what you might do in those situations to feel more in control. (For example: When you need to talk to a person, not a machine, at the bank, press zero to get a real person, not a recording; make an appointment with a personal banker or walk into the bank and speak to a representative. Let them know your needs. Be assertive.)

ANGER ALL AROUND US

Today, six-year-old Theresa observed frustrated parents yelling at and, in one case, hitting their children in the grocery store; several "popular" girls teasing and excluding another on the playground, and two boys punching a third on the school bus. She also overheard her neighbor Ms. Smith telling her parents that we should just kill all of them, referring to some race of people somewhere in the world that Theresa didn't understand; observed Mr. Simmons threatening to "kick the crap out of" the teenagers who had smashed his mailbox with a baseball bat, a father hitting his son for hitting his brother at a local restaurant, and a teacher telling a coworker that she would like to "smack Bobby's smart mouth," referring to a classmate who had talked back to the teacher in the hall. That evening she witnessed three murders on TV.

In the grocery store, Theresa's mother had shaken her head, letting Theresa know she didn't approve of parents hitting their children. When Theresa's father asked about her day at school, she told him about the teacher saying she'd like to "smack Bobby's smart mouth." Her father reminded her how violence was not a solution to problems. "What about the bad guys on TV? Don't we have to kill them?" He explained, as best he could, that TV was make-believe, but that violence on TV wasn't good either. Perhaps the most powerful lesson from Theresa's parents was when they got angry with her brother Joseph for breaking a vase when he threw a basketball in the house. They didn't raise their voices, but calmly told Joseph he would have to pay for a new vase out of the money he earned walking people's dogs.

Theresa is lucky to have parents who teach her about anger by their own healthy modeling and by talking about anger with her. However, even her parents were unaware of many of the messages Theresa received that day. It is very important to talk to children about anger, about what they see in the world, and to evaluate the effects of the behavior they observe. Otherwise, their observations become the lesson itself and they will think it's okay to tease, hit or call people names.

Check It Out

Many of the lessons that we learn about anger expression are learned from observing the interactions of those around us: family members, neighbors, community members, schoolteachers, bus drivers, coaches, etc. They teach us through the behaviors they model, the values they teach, the limits they set or the behaviors they ignore, how to deal with feelings of sadness, frustration, helplessness, anxiety, stress and anger. We learn either how to honor and respect our emotions and ourselves, or how to discount ourselves and ignore our feelings. We learn either how to honor and respect the thoughts, feelings and differences of others, or to believe there is only one right way (ours) or how to look out for "Number One." It is not only important to examine the lessons that we learned about anger and conflict resolution from our families, but also those lessons that were taught in schools, in our neighborhoods, in our broader community. In one day of little Theresa's life she could have learned:

- It is okay to exclude and bully peers.
- Hitting is acceptable when feeling frustrated.
- Respect is gained by overpowering another.
- Violence is the way to handle disagreement.

Emotional competence does not come from hiding or ignoring feelings. Everyone has feelings. Healthy people experience a full range of feelings: joy, sadness, relief, love, frustration, anger, etc. Competence comes from acknowledging feelings and realizing that we have choices regarding how to express them.

Anger can be expressed in healthy ways that lead to trust, empathy, empowerment and connection with self and others; or denied or used to overpower, manipulate, bully, disempower or control others. An example of healthy expression would be if a friend has left you waiting for an hour, and you tell her that you feel angry about it. This honestly expresses your feelings and communicates your wishes and need for respect in the relationship.

Be a detective. Spend a day being acutely aware of the anger expressions of those around you in your neighborhood, workplace or school, and community. At the end of the day, jot down what you've seen. What have you learned about the way those around you express anger, resolve conflicts and handle disagreements? Did you find any positive examples of healthy communication regarding anger? Look at the list again. What would a child have learned from the examples you have recorded? What did you learn about anger and conflict resolution from school, neighborhood and community when you were a child?

If It Bleeds, It Leads and Sells: Media, Music and Madness

Unhealthy anger expression is learned behavior. The values of power and control, aggression and dominance, and self-absorption are often reinforced through television, movies, video games and the music industry. Many violent video games use the same techniques of operant conditioning used to train soldiers to kill in Vietnam. (Grossman, 1995)

The average child today will see two hundred thousand violent acts on television before graduating from high school. In movie theaters across the nation and in front of the television at home, children are viewing details of horrible suffering and killing. They learn to associate this killing and suffering with entertainment, pleasure, "normal" behavior, and a favorite soft drink or candy bar. When children are surrounded by or shown violence, they become anxious and afraid. If this fear is not worked through and the stimulus continues, they survive by numbing, becoming desensitized to violence. "In 1999, a team of Harvard researchers looked at chronic TV watching and found it correlated positively with low public engagement and lack of sociability. It 'even correlates positively with giving the finger to people,' said David Campbell a member of the research team." (Kalle-Lasn, *Toxic TV Syndrome*, p. 143)

The good news is that we all have the power to have a positive effect on the next generation. As parents, relatives, mentors, teachers and neighbors, the good messages we give ourselves and model for children can create positive change.

Anger-obics^{SM}: Move Your Body, Shift Your Mind

Yo' Goals

What do you want to get out of this book? Check those that apply, then add any of your own.

- ❍ Gain control over my anger.
- ❍ Stop hurting the people I love with my anger.
- ❍ Feel better about myself.
- ❍ Feel happier.
- ❍ End my angry outbursts.
- ❍ Feel less powerless about my anger.
- ❍ Improve my personal relationships.
- ❍ Stop blaming myself.

- ❍ Feel stronger and more powerful.
- ❍ Know myself in a deeper way.
- ❍ Get along better with people at work.
- ❍ Stop feeling pushed around and start standing up for myself.
- ❍ Not get hurt or scared by other people's anger.
- ❍ Develop a sense of peace.

Add any others below:

- ❍ _____
- ❍ _____
- ❍ _____
- ❍ _____
- ❍ _____

Hopscotch

Get a big bag. For each anger you are carrying, pick an object in nature or around the house that reminds you of this anger. Place the object in the bag. Make sure you choose objects that won't break easily.

Picking one foot off the floor and bending your leg, grab the foot in back of you with your hand, as if you were playing hopscotch.* Pick up the bag. Hop around for a while. Imagine that this is what it's like to go about your life carrying anger, grudges and pain. You can't pick up much else, since one hand is being used to hold your foot and the other to hold the bag. You can't get around very quickly and you tire more easily.

Now let go of your foot and place it back on the floor. Walk around without the bag and with both feet on the floor. Feel your freedom. Imagine that this is the kind of change you will experience as you work through this book and your anger.

Write about the difference in the two states (hopping, walking) or draw a picture of yourself hopping and a picture of you walking. Give them each a playful title, for example, "Handicapped by Anger" and "Free Bird."

It's a Mad, Mad, Mad, Mad Word

What words do you associate with anger?

❍ frustration   ❍ rage   ❍ tension   ❍ irritability   ❍ passion   ❍ fervency   ❍ fanaticism

Add some of your own words—just free-associate and don't worry about what you write:

❍ _____   ❍ _____   ❍ _____   ❍ _____   ❍ _____

---

* Note: If this is too challenging physically, put one hand on your hip and drag the other foot around.

What are some words for how you feel when angry?

○ tense   ○ frustrated   ○ irritated   ○ fuming   ○ disappointed
○ mad   ○ mean   ○ passionate   ○ vengeful   ○ fiery

Add your own:

○ _____
○ _____
○ _____
○ _____
○ _____

Popeye Meets Deepak

This exercise demonstrates the power of our thoughts and words, using a technique called applied kinesiology. Perform this exercise with a partner. If no one is available right now, come back to it later with a friend.

Stand straight with your right arm out to the side, shoulder height, parallel to the floor. Say, "I am weak and powerless." Have your partner press your arm down towards the floor. Was it easy or difficult?

Shake out your arm and rest for a moment. Now stand the same way and say, "I am strong and powerful." Have your partner press your arm again. How did this experience differ from the first?

Consider the power of our words. Imagine the effect of telling yourself that you are powerless over your anger. Now imagine the effect of believing that you have discipline over how you express your anger and that exploring your anger will help you to become a stronger person!

MAD PAD

Well, if I called the wrong number, why did you answer the phone?

—James Thurber

> HOW MUCH MORE GRIEVOUS
> ARE THE CONSEQUENCES OF ANGER
> THAN THE CAUSES OF IT.
>
> —*Marcus Aurelius*

CHAPTER 2

LIGHT MY FIRE:
Sparks That Incite Anger

In this chapter, you will have the opportunity to understand and explore the things that provoke unhealthy anger. You will also learn how to be proactive in addressing them. There are two primary sparks that incite unhealthy anger:

- **Buttons**—those truths about us that we feel ashamed of and try to pretend don't exist (our height, weight, nationality, race, appearance, class, etc.).
- **Triggers**—experiences (sights, sounds, emotions, touch, gestures, words, etc.) that engage the pain of delayed grief or traumas from the past that we haven't resolved.

Understanding and awareness of our buttons and triggers allow us to be in control of our lives and pro-active when someone or something is likely to engage those sparks. Lack of awareness and acceptance, or denial of our buttons and triggers, can cause us to be unprepared, out of control or reactive when something or someone threatens to light our fire. When you express anger in a healthy way, you are in control of it. When you fly into a rage, your anger is in control of you.

We will also explore situations that incite your anger because you are overlooking your own needs and boundaries. As you become aware of these kinds of situations you can take steps to prepare for and, sometimes, prevent them.

WHEN YOUR BUTTONS GET PUSHED

After the birth of her first child, Joyce couldn't seem to take off the extra pounds she had gained. She had been thin all her life and felt ashamed of her weight gain, buying into the "Barbie® Doll" belief about beauty. Now when she bought clothes, she would cut the size tags off so that no one, including herself, would be reminded that she was no longer a size six. She wore big shirts to hide the few pounds she had put on, skirts with elastic waists so that she could buy a smaller size, and darker clothes to make her look thinner.

"Gained a little weight since the baby haven't you? No longer the perfect size six you used to be. If you're not careful that handsome husband of yours will be looking elsewhere," Julie laughed. "Just joking, you don't have to look so serious. You look fine."

Julie was Joyce's coworker and a bully. She had always been jealous of Joyce and loved seeing the discomfort show on her face when teased about her extra weight. Julie had found Joyce's *button* and loved the reaction she got. Joyce would look like she'd been punched, and Julie would know she had hit right on target.

Sometimes, Joyce's husband Todd, who thought she was even more beautiful since the baby was born, would tell her so, and all her anger stored at Julie and at herself for gaining those extra pounds would erupt. "You don't have to be sarcastic. I know I've gained weight. You don't have to rub it in!" She'd stomp off leaving Todd to wonder what in the world he'd said wrong.

Empowering Yourself with Self-Awareness

We all have things about ourselves that we don't like. Unfortunately, hiding those truths from ourselves gives others power over us. Every school bully, bullying coworker or boss, or relationship bully is expert at finding our buttons and pushing them. *They cannot make us victims unless we allow it.* Self-awareness and acceptance is one of our most important defenses against victimization. When we accept ourselves, warts and all, we take away the emotional stick that others may wield against us and the shaming messages we sometimes use to bludgeon ourselves. For instance: Did Joyce gain weight after her pregnancy? Yes. Did the extra pounds she gained mean that she was unworthy or unattractive? No. She was comparing herself to a distorted model of perfection sold on toy-store shelves and on magazine covers. Perhaps she would have benefited from a trip to the art museum where she could feast on the breathtaking paintings of mothers and children that have been revered throughout history. Those mothers certainly do not resemble Barbie.

Taking Away the Stick

Sometimes when others tease us, our friends and family try to make us feel better by pretending our buttons (our race, ethnicity, weight, etc.) don't exist. Rather than helping us come to terms with our buttons, they want us to ignore them. This does not lead to self-acceptance and strength. Instead, it increases vulnerability and victimization. For example, Roberto was teased relentlessly at school for being Puerto Rican. His parents, in their attempt to help, told him, "You're just like everyone else," instead of arming the child with awareness and pride in his culture. Is he like everyone else? No. The youth who teased him were blond and blue-eyed.

An example of a child who was taught to take away the stick appears in *Bully-Proofing Your School* by

C. K. Garrity. The child had been continually teased about her culture. Instead of being taught to deny who she was, she was taught to feel pride in her culture and given tools to take the power away from the bullies. The next time she was teased, she came prepared with information about her country of origin. When the bully began to tease her she replied, "You know, you have shown so much interest in my heritage that I thought you might like to read some books on the subject." She did not pull out a "stick" to use on the bully or herself. Instead, she took the stick away. (Garrity et al., 1994)

Truth and Fiction

List your buttons and the messages you give yourself or others give you about them on your *Mad Pad*. List your reaction to these messages, the truth and fiction in each message, and things you can do to empower yourself and take away the stick others use to hurt you or you use to hurt yourself. Examples:

Name	Bullying Statement	Button	Fact or Fiction	Message You Give Yourself	True or False
Aaron	"You're a shrimp, and shrimps are wimps."	I'm short.	Fact	I'm not as good as other men.	False
Sam	"Indians are lazy drunks."	I'm Native American.	Fact	Indians are dirty, lazy drunks.	False
Ellen	"Hey, fatso."	I'm overweight.	Fact	I am ugly and unlovable.	False

Truth or Falsehood in Message

(Aaron) Real truth: Competent, talented and strong men come in all heights. I am very capable in my job and a good father.

(Sam) Real truth: Historically, some of our greatest leaders, talented artists and role models have been Native American and First Nations people. Some of the greatest contributions to our society have come from my people. Some people from all races are alcoholic or suffer from depression.

(Ellen) Real truth: I do not fit the stereotype of body perfection that is sold as beauty, but I am not "ugly." I have had difficulty overcoming the stereotype, but yesterday I saw a movie where the beautiful heroine was full-figured like me. I am a good friend and a talented artist. I am loved and respected by many people and am a kind and lovable person.

How I Have Reacted When My Buttons Have Been Pushed

(Aaron) I have tended to react by being overly sensitive about my height and defensive about my strength and capabilities. I have overreacted to any constructive criticism and reacted with outbursts of anger. I have occasionally bullied coworkers to make myself feel more powerful.

(Sam) When my buttons are pushed, I often withdraw and isolate myself.

(Ellen) When my buttons are pushed, I tend to go through a cycle: I put myself down and call myself names, comparing myself to others and coming up short. I force myself to go on strict diets; I've been on hundreds. After I've been on a diet for a while, all I can think about is food. Soon I binge, become depressed and promise myself it will work next time. The focus of my life is always on food one way or another. Even my first awareness of people around me is whether they're fat or thin, not who they are, and in my mind I put down the ones who are overweight just like I put myself down. Sometimes I joke about my weight. I also realize that when I'm hurt or angry, I eat.

How I Can Take Away the Stick

(Aaron) I need to accept my strengths, talents and capabilities. I can take a few hours to observe the differences in people's body types as well as become more aware of competent, talented and strong people in all walks of life who have been short of stature. I need to listen more carefully to what people are actually

saying, rather than what I hear when my buttons are pushed. I need to stop bullying others. It gives me a feeling of power temporarily, but later I feel worse. I need to start by letting people know that I sometimes tend to be a bully and ask the few people in my life whom I trust to confront me on my behavior.

(Sam) I want to become more aware of the strengths of my culture. A friend suggested that I read *Indian Givers* by Jack Weatherford, a book about the contributions of Native American and First Nations people. Maybe I could copy down some of the contributions on a sheet of paper to give people who tease me about my culture. I want to stop focusing on unfavorable statistics and surround myself with supportive and positive people. I need to tell a few trusted friends about my buttons, that sometimes I withdraw, but now I want to reach out instead.

(Ellen) I want to stop making my weight the center of my life and work toward balance. I want to accept my body and begin treating it with respect. I need to focus on health, not weight; on exercise and becoming aware when I'm full; on developing healthy eating habits, not diets. I need to focus on the parts of myself that are capable and talented, and allow myself to take in the respect, love and appreciation of those around me, rather than minimize the positive feedback I get. When I feel put down, I need to seek out support rather than isolate myself. I want to start dressing as if I respect myself and my body. I want to ask for support from others to express my anger rather than swallow it. I want to accept all of myself, including my weight, rather than join others in putting myself down.

CORE ISSUES AND TRIGGERS

Triggers—experiences in the present that bring up unresolved hurts or traumas of the past—can provoke intense anger in seconds. Reacting to triggers is like walking around with a loaded emotional gun inside. Triggers are the major cause of unhealthy anger expression. Triggers can be:

- Sights (the color of a room or the house you grew up in)
- Sounds (a baby's cry or raised voices)
- Touch (being approached from behind or unexpected hugs)
- Smells (cologne or perfume, beer on someone's breath)
- Facial expressions (a blank stare, fear, sadness)
- Emotional states (anger, fear, powerlessness, needs)
- Styles of communication (lying, whining, slurred speech)
- Dates, seasons, holidays (Christmas, birthdays, death anniversaries)

Even our children's ages and birthdays can trigger thoughts and feelings from the past that affect our present responses by causing us to overreact (start a fight, fly into a rage or act out) or underreact (become depressed, freeze or shut down). For instance, being stuck in a traffic jam might trigger a feeling of helplessness that was experienced at another time of life. For many, helplessness was a feeling that was forbidden, ridiculed or punished. The helpless feeling is bypassed, and the result is road rage.

Unfriendly Ghosts: Triggers and Responses

Ned grew up in a family and, indeed, a culture where men were supposed to be tough and independent without needing comfort or support. When he was frightened, sad or in need of nurture, his father would tease him relentlessly calling him a "mama's boy" or telling him he had to "cut the apron strings" if he was to be *a man*. When he showed fear or sensitivity in elementary school, he would be teased by the other boys. He learned quickly that to be a man meant being strong, without needs or fears, and definitely never crying.

Gloria grew up in a family where opinions were not to be expressed and any show of anger could result in being sent to your room or ignored. Girls could cry, sometimes sulk, but never be angry.

When Ned and Gloria married, it was like a match made in a haunted castle. He could show anger but never cry; she could cry but not express opinions or be angry. They triggered each other regularly. Her tears triggered his feelings of helplessness, which then triggered his rage. His anger triggered her anger, which then triggered her tears. If he felt overwhelmed or tired, instead of asking for help, he would be angry. If he came home late or failed to help with the children, she would isolate herself and sulk. It was a very uncomfortable dance with breaks for distant small talk concerning the day-to-day running of the house or the children. Theirs became a house of loud silence.

Disengaging Your Triggers

Frequently unresolved feelings from the past get mixed up with feelings in the present. When you are feeling more emotion than a situation warrants (becoming enraged when your partner squeezes the toothpaste from the middle) you can safely assume that you've been triggered. When we can't talk our feelings out, we tend to act them out. In order to avoid overreacting or underreacting, we need to be aware and accountable for our personal triggers. We need to reach out, talk it out and not act it out.

When you become aware of anger triggers, you may also learn where the triggers originate. Then you can work on them by deactivating the loaded areas of your life. Gloria and Ned were at the point of threatening each other with divorce when they began working on their triggers and, instead, kicked out the ghosts in their castle. They were able to learn a great deal by outlining their triggers, as illustrated in the following chart. This activity involves listing the trigger, the resulting emotional response, the physical response, the behavioral response, the feelings blocked by the behavior response, and finally, the unresolved grief, trauma or shame behind the trigger. You may have difficulty filling in all of the areas listed. For example, many people know what feelings they are blocking but not the unresolved ghosts from the past. Others may know the grief, trauma or shame but not the emotions they are blocking. Just do your best.

Gloria's Recent Triggers and Responses/Ned's Recent Triggers and Responses

Person	Trigger	Immediate Emotional Response	Physical Response
Gloria	*Ned's Anger*	*Anxiety*	*Shaky inside, stomachache*
Ned	**Gloria's tears**	**Anger**	**Tense, tight**

Person	Behavioral Response	Feelings Blocked by Behavior Response
Gloria	*Broke down in tears*	*Anger*
Ned	**Yelled at Gloria and walked out**	**Helplessness, powerlessness**

Person	Unresolved Trauma, Shame or Delayed Grief
Gloria	*Being isolated and shamed for expressing opinions or normal anger throughout her growing up years*
Ned	**Being shamed throughout childhood for feelings of helplessness, powerlessness and sensitivity**

You can explore your own triggers, responses and core issues in the *Anger-obics*™ section of this chapter.

OVERLOOKING YOUR NEEDS AND BOUNDARIES

When Katie came home from work on Friday night, she was dead tired. She tended to overwork, often doing more than her share, covering for those who didn't seem to be able to carry their load. All day she had been looking forward to a long bath complete with candles. At last, time to relax, time just for her.

Katie had just put her toe in the warm, fragrant water when the phone rang. She tried to make herself let the answering machine pick it up. She couldn't. What if it was an important call? But, alas, it was Teresa, her long-suffering friend who always had a crisis. Did she ever call her when she wanted to share good news or to ask Katie about her life? No—another crisis with yet another person out to get her. Katie endured the call, stopping the long diatribe to interject a possible suggestion here and there, which, Teresa pointed out, would never work. Oh well, her friend just needed to vent. That's what friends are for, right?

An hour and a half later Katie had emptied half the water in the tub, added more hot water and replenished the fragrant bubbles, when the phone rang yet again. *Ignore it! Ignore it!* She couldn't do it. Now it was George, another friend in need. "Katie, I know this is short notice, but I have a business trip tomorrow and I forgot to call the kennel to board Bruiser. Could you be a great friend and take care of him for me?"

Damn, she really didn't want to do it. She'd taken care of Bruiser twice in the last month because George couldn't seem to order his life enough to call the kennel. The last time, Bruiser had eaten her favorite slippers. She really didn't like the "thoughtless" animal that seemed to be as irresponsible as his owner. "Sure, bring him over in a couple of hours."

"Thanks, you're such a good friend. What would I do without you? The thing is I've got to pack. Didn't get to it last night and I have to leave in a couple of hours. Could you be a jewel and pick him up?"

Not this time, she thought. Hadn't she promised herself that she wouldn't take care of the rowdy mutt again? She was beginning to hate the dog. She had yelled hysterically at him when he peed on her rug, then locked him in the basement. "Sure," she replied. "I'll stop by in about an hour."

"Could you be a peach and make it a half hour? I've got to run past the dry cleaners on my way to the airport." Yes, indeed, that was Katie, "a real peach."

Something's Got to Give, Something's Got to Give, Something's Got to Give

No bath for Katie! The chance of Bruiser getting compassionate treatment is nil, and George and Teresa will soon be history.

Katie's pattern is an all-too-familiar one for many. When we don't protect our own boundaries, we often store anger, exploding all of a sudden (in this case on undeserving Bruiser) and/or collecting reasons to abruptly end friendships. In Katie's case, she has a history of suddenly feeling taken for granted and ending friendships abruptly after saying "yes" one too many times. The numerous friends Katie has suddenly left in the dust have no idea what happened: friends one day, frozen out the next.

While George and Teresa certainly have tested the limits of friendship, Katie, for her part, has never let them know that she, too, has limits. First Katie must learn to trust herself to protect herself and her boundaries; then she can learn to trust others. When we don't set our own personal boundaries, sometimes we slowly build walls, abruptly exit relationships, justify sudden rages when demands get too much, or get worn out and sick. The illness or exit is the only way we finally take a break.

As we become aware of our triggers, buttons and boundaries, we can begin to undo our negative behavior patterns, feel more control of our lives, and gain new respect for ourselves and others. On your *Mad Pad* you may want to list those people in your life who overstep limits or ask you for too much. Are there ways you could politely turn excessive requests down? Call up a friend who respects boundaries and brainstorm what you might say to one of your "over-steppers."

Anger-obics^{SM}: Move Your Body, Shift Your Mind

Gratitude Attitude

This is a useful exercise for feeling calm. It may be used before other exercises or when you want to calm down.

Stand straight or sit comfortably in a chair with your back straight. If possible, try not to lean back in the chair for support, but sit in the forward part of the chair. Plant your feet flat on the floor or ground.

Close your eyes and notice your breathing. Become more aware of your body sitting or standing. Observe the sensation of your feet connecting to the floor. Notice your hands in your lap or on your knees. How do your clothes feel against your skin? Do you notice any sensation in your face? Bring your attention to the area around your heart. In your heart feel gratitude for the home that Earth provides, for the food that nourishes you, for a person you love and anything else that makes you grateful.

Whoa, Trigger

People are set off by different triggers. It can be very helpful to know what triggers an unhealthy anger response for you. Then you can begin to find ways to deal with the particular situation (such as getting help beforehand, avoiding some triggers, preparing for the trigger). Below our examples, make a list of some of the things that most trigger your anger, along with your unhealthy anger response:

Sights	Unhealthy Anger Response
• My partner's clothes strewn about the floor	• I yell at my partner
• _____	• _____
• _____	• _____
• _____	• _____

Sounds	Unhealthy Anger Response
• A child crying	• I feel helpless, and then scream at my children
• _____	• _____
• _____	• _____
• _____	• _____

Touch	Unhealthy Anger Response
• Being touched from behind	• I want to strike out
• _____	• _____

Touch *(continued)*

- _____
- _____

Unhealthy Anger Response *(continued)*

- _____
- _____

Facial Expressions

- Rolling eyes
- _____
- _____
- _____

Unhealthy Anger Response

- I start a fight
- _____
- _____
- _____

Emotional States

- Vulnerability or fear
- _____
- _____
- _____

Unhealthy Anger Response

- I fly into a rage
- _____
- _____
- _____

Style of Communication	Unhealthy Anger Response
• Lying or whining	• I punish or scream at my kids
• _____	• _____
• _____	• _____
• _____	• _____

Dates, Seasons, Holidays	Unhealthy Anger Response
• Christmas	• I feel depressed and get drunk
• _____	• _____
• _____	• _____
• _____	• _____

Whoa, Trigger II

Becoming aware of your triggers and how you behave when triggered are the first two steps to adopting healthier behavior. The next step is to develop a plan for action which includes:

- Feeling the feelings without necessarily reacting to them
- Coming up with a plan of action
- Taking concrete steps to deactivate your triggers

Below is a sample action plan. On the following page, choose one or more triggers that are prominent in your life and develop an action plan for them:

Trigger & Behavior	Action Plan
Rage/scream when stuck in traffic	• Cool off before getting in car.
	• Picture myself in traffic and remaining calm, before I start driving.
	• Listen to calming music while driving.
	• Work toward accepting feelings of helplessness.
	• Resolve issues underlying the anger.

Trigger & Behavior	Action Plan
• _____	• _____
• _____	• _____
• _____	• _____
• _____	• _____
• _____	• _____
• _____	• _____
• _____	• _____
• _____	• _____
• _____	• _____
• _____	• _____
• _____	• _____
• _____	• _____
• _____	• _____

Now add ways you can protect yourself against sabotage:

Ways I Could Sabotage Myself	Guards Against Self-Sabotage
• Getting into the car when I'm already triggered	• Carpool with coworker
• _____	• _____
• _____	• _____
• _____	• _____
• _____	• _____

Ways I Could Sabotage Myself	Guards Against Self-Sabotage
• _____	• _____
• _____	• _____
• _____	• _____
• _____	• _____

Note: The above exercise is from *Boiling Point: The Workbook* (Middelton-Moz, 2000, 42–45).

Emotion in Motion

Often, we feel a release when we physically respond to the emotion of anger. In fact, our body's anger response is designed for "fight or flight," a very physical response. Here is a way to express the anger physically without throwing or breaking anything!

1. Put on music that for you expresses the emotion of anger.
2. Think about something that made you mildly angry recently. If you can't think of anything, pick a situation in appendix C.
3. Turn your anger into a gesture or movement as you listen to the angry music.
4. Allow yourself to move with the music.
5. Has the feeling of anger in your body changed at all? How does it feel? Do you notice a difference in your feelings or perception of the situation after moving?
6. If you don't notice a change or your anger has increased, allow yourself to come to a more neutral place by playing music that you find soothing. Create a physical action that reinforces the feeling of the music: a gesture or a movement.

You can make notes here:

_____

_____

_____

_____

Think Thank

Do you often find yourself thinking anger-provoking thoughts? Do you focus on how specific people in your life are wronging you?

Many philosophers and spiritual teachers suggest that our thoughts become our reality. If we constantly tell ourselves that people are taking advantage of us, we will find that they are. One way to begin to get out of this rut is to identify the anger-provoking thoughts we find ourselves thinking and replace them with healthier thoughts. When you find yourself in a familiar angry thought (one you think often), jot it down. Perhaps you can even think of some of those thoughts right now. Is there a way you can turn an angry thought into a positive thought?

Example:

Angry Thought	Positive Thought
Sonia is always late and making me wait for her; she must not value my time.	When Sonia is late, I am going to focus on what I need to do for myself. If I cannot wait, I will go on with my plans. I am responsible for how I react to Sonia's lateness.
People always want something from me; they must think I'm a pushover.	People often ask me for favors. Maybe they trust me. However, I can choose to say, "yes" or "no" or offer a middle ground.

Write your examples below:

Angry Thought	Positive Thought

MAD PAD

MOST POWERFUL IS HE WHO HAS
HIMSELF IN HIS OWN POWER.

—*Seneca*

NOTHING SHAMEFUL ABOUT ANGER . . .
SOMETIMES IT'S THE ONLY SANE AND
LOGICAL AND MORAL REACTION.

—*Carl Hiaasen*
Sick Puppy

CHAPTER 3

BAD COMPANY:
Unhealthy Anger

In this chapter you learn to recognize common "styles" of expressing (or not expressing) anger. By understanding the motivations that underlie each style, and by identifying your own style or styles, you will be better able to deal effectively with expression of anger, in others and in yourself. In this chapter, you will also increase your understanding of rage: anger out of control.

CONFRONTING UNHEALTHY ANGER STYLES

Anger is a normal emotion, yet many people in our society are afraid of healthy anger and are taught from a young age not to feel or express it. Many people are socialized to "be nice" and not to "make waves," while others are taught to "fight back" rather than to allow themselves normal feelings of sadness or vulnerability. Anger often ceases to be a healthy, constructive emotion and becomes destructive to ourselves or others and to our ability to build healthy, lasting relationships. Anger may come out sideways: through hurtful humor, clenched jaws, grinding teeth, procrastination, temper tantrums, memory loss, chronic lateness, righteousness, gossip, twitching eyes, irritability, depression or rage.

Sometimes the messages we receive about healthy emotions instruct us to hide our feelings from others and from ourselves. We learn to show one thing on the outside while experiencing another on the inside. We learn to present masks to the world that conceal our true feelings.

Unhealthy Anger as a Block to Emotional Health

Unhealthy anger serves as a defense:

- Unhealthy anger keeps us from dealing with the source of our fears.
- Unhealthy anger prevents us from working through grief and loss.
- Unhealthy anger keeps us from dealing with the messages that continue our shame.
- Unhealthy anger keeps us from examining emotional hurts and feelings of powerlessness and vulnerability.
- Unhealthy anger stops us from resolving conflicts and problem solving.
- Unhealthy anger keeps us isolated.
- Unhealthy anger "protects" us from the vulnerability of intimacy.

The Masks We Wear

We are frequently unaware that our behaviors form patterns. There are many styles of unhealthy anger expression. There are unique strategies for effectively dealing with each style.

Whining Winnie

Whining Winnie really drains your energy. Sometimes her voice sounds like anger and frustration being forced through a straw. Forget suggestions to help her with her endless complaints.

She'll tell you why each carefully thought-out solution won't work. After her list of complaints you're so frustrated that you're ready to jog until you drop.

Whine-not, Dear Winnie

Whining Winnie has trouble with limits, so give her some. If she interrupts your work, set a time later to talk. Set a time limit for listening to complaints. Be honest that you feel frustrated listening to the same complaints repeatedly. Tell her you would like to spend time with her when she's feeling content and not only when she's upset about something. When she complains, don't try to find the solutions for her. You will only become frustrated when she tells you why nothing will work. Put the ball in her court: "I hear you're angry about _____. What are you going to do about it?" If she continues to complain, ask the same question again. If she is not interested in solutions, she'll tire of your suggesting that she empower herself and she'll complain to someone else.

Temperamental Tito

Temperamental Tito throws tantrums. You don't need to guess if he's angry. What brought all this on? His tantrums seem to come out of nowhere. He doesn't stop at giving you reasons for his anger. It's a twenty-minute shout-fest filled with foot-stomping and finger-pointing. Forget about trying to get a word in. Then, he's over it, back to his calm, quiet, overly serene self, and you're left feeling shell-shocked.

Encouraging Temperamental Tito to Toe the Line

Approach Tito to see if he will agree to the rules of conscious conflict [chapter 8]. If so, you may proceed from there to make the relationship healthier. If he does not agree, let him know that you cannot be around him when he yells, calls names or throws things. When Tito raises his voice or becomes emotionally abusive, tell him you are not comfortable with his behavior and need a "time-out." Then leave. It is important to set limits so that you are not exposing yourself to his hurtful behaviors.

Talk to him when he has calmed down. Let him know that you are concerned about his behavior, your relationship and his health. Titos can suffer from heart disease as a result of holding in and then exploding. Tito would benefit from seeing a physician who understands the toll these tantrums take.

Perfect Patrice

Perfect Patrice is always right. In arguments, she relentlessly tries to convince you that you're wrong. If only you saw it her way, everything would be fine. Not only is she never wrong, but she works harder, loves more, is a much better friend and is never appreciated enough.

Staying Present with Perfect Patrice

When dealing with Perfect Patrice, point out that you are not attacking her, just expressing your needs, desires and individuality. If you can, give her positive strokes and the appreciation she works for. When she feels valued, it will be easier for her to hear your critical feedback. Some of the conscious conflict tools in chapter 8 will help you such as: "When you _____
I feel _____ I need _____"
statements. Don't get caught up in "prove it." Effectively dealing with Perfect Patrice is a bit like being a traffic guard on Boundary Street: "You make your choices. I make my choices." "You have your thoughts and opinions, I have my thoughts and opinions." "You're responsible for your self-esteem, I'm responsible for my self-esteem." (Middelton-Moz and Zawadski, 2000)

Stacy the Stamp Collector

Stacy the Stamp Collector can tell you everything you've done to offend her for the last twenty years. She remembers every slight or injustice perpetrated against her and will gladly throw it at your feet in a disagreement. The hoarded resentments serve as protection against further wounds to a vulnerable self. She and Perfect Patrice are tight; one rarely goes anywhere without the other.

Stopping Stacy the Stamp Collector Before She Throws the Book at You

Stacy needs to see herself as "good person," "easygoing," and "reasonable," because inside she feels insecure, inadequate and angry. She fears abandonment and is always waiting for "the other shoe to drop" so she "walks on egg shells," "is pleasing," and compromises her wishes and needs. Stacy fears conflict and intimacy, and protects herself from both by collecting resentments like stamps in a book. When the book is full, or she feels cornered, she turns the book in on a guilt-free tirade, ending a relationship or friendship, or as proof of her "goodness."

Don't settle for her "I don't know, you decide" or "it's all right, I don't mind," if you want to keep a friendship or continue a relationship with her. Ask her to be clear about her needs, wishes, likes, dislikes and feelings in the present. When she begins to trot out everything you've done since 1901, remind her that the disagreement being discussed is in the present and that she is responsible for bringing up disappointments or resentments as they happen. If she continues, remind her again that you want to work on the present disagreement. If she can't stop hurling the book of stamps at you, take a break and resume the conversation when the book has been put down.

Continue to remind Stacy that she is in charge of stating her needs and feelings, and you are in charge of stating yours, emphasizing that neither of you is capable of "mind-reading."

Bullying Boris

Bullying Boris intimidates everyone in order to get what he wants. When you fight with him you lose; when you break down in tears, you lose. He's loud, self-righteous, sarcastic, unpredictable and gets his way most of the time. At work, he's the boss (or coworker) from hell.

Convincing Bullying Boris to Behave

Bullying Boris is an expert in intimidation techniques. He repeatedly uses behaviors that have worked for him in the past to gain power and control over others and get his own way. He has been perfecting his skills for years and depends upon eliciting confusion, fear or feelings of powerlessness in his targets. Rendering his targets helpless or forcing them to lose control of their tempers enables Bullying Boris to gain control of the situation.

Stand up to Boris but avoid fighting with him. Be assertive, not demanding. Look him in the eye; use confident body language; focus on the behavior you wish to have stopped without using labels; stop him from interrupting you; say it simply; avoid absolutes like "you always" or "you never"; be direct.

Always get support for yourself. Don't personalize Bully Boris's bad behavior, and carefully choose whether to confront him alone or with others. If you have a history of having been bullied by Boris, if he is in a position of power, or if you have reason to believe that his behavior could escalate his abuse, make sure that supportive others are standing with you or that you are a part of a well-planned group confrontation. (Middelton-Moz and Zawadski, 2000)

Remember, Bullying Boris usually depends on an audience for his power. Don't allow yourself to be one of the "silent majority" that he uses as a tool to bully.

Gwen the Gossip

Gwen the Gossip says "nothing's wrong" with a smile on her face. Watch your back. Monday morning you may return to work to find out she's told the whole office that you made a mistake in front of your client and were making eyes at a coworker at the office party.

Putting the Lid on Gwen the Gossip

Gwen's gossip and put-downs come from her own feelings of inadequacy. Don't personalize her put-downs and don't let her bully you. Confront her directly: Tell her what you heard and ask her if she said it. Expect Gwen to deny the gossip and to blame the misunderstanding on the person who passed it on to you. Respond by saying, "Great. I will let _____ know what you said." Look Gwen in the eye and tell her that if she has any concerns or perceptions about your life you expect her to say things directly to you first.

Don't let Gossiping Gwen involve you in bullying another. If she gossips to you say, "I'm not comfortable hearing you speak about _____.
Please let _____ know what you're feeling directly."

Violent Vince

Violent Vince is bad news. He throws glass bottles and breaks chairs. Occasionally he hits someone. But it's never his fault: "She made me hit her. She deserved it." Even though his rages are always *someone else's fault,* he's usually sorry until the next time.

Setting Limits on Violent Vince

If you are in a relationship or are friends with someone who is abusive or violent, emotionally, mentally or physically, insist that he or she get help, if you are to stay in the relationship. You don't deserve to be the recipient of abuse or violence. There is no conflict, argument, difference of opinion or behavior that justifies physical or emotional violence. Emotional violence always accompanies physical violence—in the form of put-downs, intimidation, limiting the personal freedom of a partner, threats, stalking, public humiliation or continual unsupported accusations. Domestic violence isn't about anger, but the "need" to control others. It is brought about by the inability to express vulnerability, powerlessness and fear. A partner or friend with access to a range of emotions, including healthy anger, isn't physically or emotionally violent.

If you can't be safe in this relationship, it may be time to leave with the support of others, or take a hiatus until Violent Vince can get help. If he is directing violence towards your child, call for help (police, social services) immediately. Remember, Violent Vince will most likely apologize afterwards. The apology or promise that it will never happen again may sound sincere because Violent Vince has a system of rationalization, denying the seriousness of his behavior. Physically or emotionally violent partners don't change their behavior without external consequences and treatment. It is extremely important for you to develop a supportive network that includes friends, understanding family members, trained advocates, counselors, etc. It is critical that you not place yourself in a dangerous situation with someone who is physically and/or emotionally violent. (Middelton-Moz, 1999)

DEPRESSION, ADDICTION, COMPULSION AND ILLNESS

In addition to the "masks" above, people wear other "masks" that you may not realize are rooted in anger. Sad Sal, Vanishing Vanessa and Al the Addict are all repressing their anger.

Sad Sal appears to be breathing from the neck up while her stomach is churning like a cement mixer. While she seems to be sitting in a relaxed position, she's exerting so much physical and emotional control that if you were to carefully pull the chair out from under her, she would comfortably remain in midair. The anger that Sal only briefly experiences is immediately internalized. Sal becomes depressed when angry. She's unreachable; she isolates and might take to her bed for weeks.

Vanishing Vanessa protects herself by being invisible—thereby avoiding conflict or self-exposure. If you ask, "Are you hungry?" the reply is, "I don't know. Are you?" If you ask, "What would you like to eat?" she answers, "I don't know. What are you in the mood for?" Vanishing Vanessa and Sad Sal are pals and can be seen everywhere together.

Al the Addict turns to drugs, booze, bakeries or Bingo when angry or depressed, or uses his addiction as an excuse to release anger. "You know I wouldn't have been out of control if I wasn't drinking."

The Traffic Jam of Depression

Depression is like having feelings caught in a traffic jam. Anger, shame, sadness, fear, helplessness and even joy seem paralyzed. Feelings need to move in order for the emotional traffic to flow. Anger, shame, fear, sadness and helplessness that cannot be expressed will become depressed.

Unfortunately, many of us have learned to keep our feelings inside, to shut up and take it, to appear "strong" by keeping all of our pain inside. When we are shame-bound, it becomes hard to express normal and healthy feelings of sadness or anger without shame. Depressed individuals frequently suffer from an accumulation of loneliness, hopelessness, shame, anger and/or helplessness that is paralyzing.

Elements of Depression

- **Shame and Self-Hate:** Many of us feel ashamed to express confusion, pain, anger, helplessness and fear. We develop a derivative sense of self—we're "nobody until somebody loves us," and love means being strong, avoiding conflict and/or being continually pleasing and happy. If we learned that the expression of normal anger and sadness is the antithesis of love and a destroyer of love, we learn to repress and feel shame about otherwise healthy emotions. Then we hate ourselves for being depressed because depression isn't *lovable* either. When individuals are continually shamed, they frequently: (1) humiliate others (anger-out); (2) give themselves messages that are hurtful, shameful and humiliating (anger-in); and/or (3) form relationships with others where humiliation continues (anger-in).
- **Isolation:** When we hide our feelings of pain and anger, we develop a strong sense of isolation, which increases depression. Without others, we cannot begin to dislodge the traffic jam of feelings. If we don't talk or write it out, we will act it in or act it out. With increased pain, many of us are becoming more and more isolated from each other. Many people feel isolated even in a crowd. We have stopped saying the *N* word (need). We need each other and often don't recognize how much we need each other.
- **Learned Helplessness:** An individual's perceived control over experiences produces heightened self-esteem and guards against depression. A depressed person believes that any action taken on his/her own behalf is futile. He or she perceives that success is not determined by skills, actions, behavior, effort or performance. An individual who is repeatedly confronted with trauma will feel intense fear, learned helplessness and resulting depression. Another who is given what she or he wants without working for it is conditioned to understand that what is received has little to do with his or her behaviors, actions, abilities or effort; and in today's world of runaway technology countless people feel that their lives are out of

their control and that their actions have little to do with outcome. Learned helplessness and depression often go hand in hand.

- **The Body Has a Head:** Imbalances of serotonin, norepenephrine and dopamine can result from psychological or physiological trauma, the triggering of unresolved grief, self-defeating thoughts and/or environmental stress. When clinical depression is present, the use of medication may be a necessary part of effective treatment. A common misperception is that medication solves the problem. It may change the depressive response, but the underlying causes of the biochemical symptoms are still present. Once off the medication, a person will need to have changed the way in which he or she responds to the underlying issues. This is why therapy is a crucial complement to taking medication.

Compulsions: Dime Stores, Exercise, Sex, Bakeries, Business, Booze and Bingo

It had been a wretched Friday at the office. Bill the Bully blasted everyone in sight, Tito's tantrums were terrifying and Gwen the gossip goaded Priscilla. Camille and Cameron the Communicators stood up to their intimidators, did their *Anger-obics*ᔆᔆᴹ exercises, wrote in their *Mad Pad*s, and settled into a fun-filled weekend with friends and family. Unfortunately many others carried their anger home: Shawn the Shopper spent an enormous amount of money at the mall on the way home from work and was later too depressed to move off the sofa; Olive the Overeater stopped at the bakery, ate ten huge cookies then hated herself for it; Evan the Exerciser was still seen running around the block on Sunday morning; William the Workaholic worked all weekend; Seth and Simone the Sexaholics had sex at the park-and-ride, then hightailed it home to the partners they loved, and spent the weekend ashamed and terrified that they might have been seen; Al the Addict was drunk all weekend, didn't make it to work that week and was finally fired on Friday; and Bernice, who lost most of her savings at Bingo three nights running, was bummed and broke on Monday.

Compulsive and addictive behaviors such as overeating, compulsive exercise, gambling, spending, workaholism, relationship addiction, and drug and alcohol abuse are born of intense craving for nurturing, affection, connection and personal power. Under the surface of compulsive behaviors lies an insecure, frightened and angry individual crying out in loneliness, isolation, helplessness, fear and anger. Compulsive behaviors represent an attempt at survival, security, satisfaction, identity and safety. The compulsions become replacements for nurturing; the means to diminish anxiety and insecurity, and experience brief pleasure and gratification; the means to repress anger and hostility; and an avenue to find temporary security. Compulsive behaviors represent the paradox of both an overwhelming desire for connectedness and a fear of intimacy and conflict. The spending, hoarding, sex, compulsive work, etc., reflect an effort to protect oneself against overwhelming feelings of helplessness, hopelessness and fear of abandonment should emotions held in check be released.

Frequently in our attempts to stop compulsive behaviors we isolate the behavior, ignoring the internal fear and pain. Diets don't work in the long run, because they disregard the underlying emotions of compulsive eating. Like the old cartoon where an object is pounded into one part of the lawn only to pop up in another, behavioral approaches frequently result in stopping one compulsion only to have another take its place.

Most compulsive behaviors are followed by continued messages of self-castigation and depression. Anger is once again turned on the self, continuing the cycle of self-hate and compulsive behavior. The gambling, the overeating, the spending are seen as weakness, a lack of will, thus pointing another shaming finger at an already shame-bound self, when what is needed is an honest mirror, someone to listen and support to find one's own voice.

PASSIVE AGGRESSION

Osman learned early in his relationship with Mariam that if he angered her he would be eating burnt food on her nights to cook. When it was her turn to do the laundry, his underwear would be pink and his favorite white shirts would end up green. She was never *angry,* but she really was angry.

Individuals who express their anger "passive-aggressively" do just that; they are simultaneously aggressive and passive. Being in a relationship with a passive-aggressive is like hugging a big, soft down pillow full of thorns. The pillow looks so inviting that you have difficulty believing the thorns are there until one goes through your ear.

Passive-aggressive individuals learn early in life not to openly express resentment and/or anger. Often they learn that they must be a "good girl" or "good boy." They begin to harbor resentment at constantly needing to be good and outwardly compliant in order to maintain acceptance and connection with those they depend on for sustenance. They learn not to confront situations directly but rather to achieve some measure of control through manipulation and oppositional patterns of behavior. In other words, their anger comes out sideways.

Significant others, family members, coworkers and friends of the passive-aggressive person go through an entire gamut of feelings. First come feelings of frustration, helplessness, inadequacy and lack of control, followed by anger and often guilt. All these emotions are the very feelings that individuals with a passive-aggressive style struggle against experiencing, especially anger. Isn't it convenient that these *in-and-out* individuals find others to experience their feelings for them? (Middelton-Moz, 1999)

A passive-aggressive person may consistently arrive late, break promises, give unclear messages (setting you up to fail) or leave a mess. Be honest with the person concerning what about their behavior bothers you and how you feel. Present consequences for the behavior: "Next time I'm not going to wait." Don't take the behavior personally—it may seem personal, but her behavior and emotions don't belong to you.

In dealing with a passive-aggressive, know what pushes your buttons. Explore your own feelings, with or without acting on them, and stop exploring hers. For instance, if you are often kept waiting for her and you have obligations, stop trying to figure out why she's habitually late, and get on with your life. Let her deal with her feelings. Ask yourself if you are willing to carry someone else's emotional baggage. If not, leave and she'll be forced to carry her own.

THE RAGES

- "I have the right of way here, you jerk! Get out of my way or I'll have to make you!"
- "Now you listen to me, you bimbo, I'm a million-mile flyer and I want the plane to take off right now!"
- "If you freeze up one more time or I see one more error message, you piece of junk, you're out the window!"
- "Miss that ball again and I'm gonna come down there and beat the crap outta you!"

These raging voices are becoming increasingly common in our homes, on the roadways and skyways, in office buildings where computers have been known to be hurled out of windows, and at sporting events where fans turn violent. Raging is becoming so common that we even have names for these episodes: "road rage," "sky rage," "computer rage" and "sports rage."

Anger isn't healthy unless it's expressed and released in ways that lead to appropriate action and/or resolution. Unfortunately, anger too often bursts forth in inappropriate ways much like a balloon that is pumped too full of air until it finally pops. Stored anger and frustration too often find an outlet while their host is driving a car, working at the computer, waiting at a ticket counter at an airport or sparring with a partner after a frustrating day at work.

Increased Powerlessness

Many people tell us that they feel little power in their lives, that they are less and less able to influence most aspects of their day-to-day lives:

- "I don't talk to a person, I talk to a computer."
- "There are more cars on the road, more construction, more traffic jams and more noise."
- "Both of us work full-time jobs, but with rising costs, we still can't get ahead."

These people are expressing a sense of helplessness. They feel incapable of choice in an impersonal world. Michael Lerner refers to this feeling of insignificance as "surplus powerlessness." He states that "treating people badly is often the result of our previous surplus powerlessness, particularly our belief that everyone will always be hurting each other so we'd better do it first." (Lerner, 1986, p.5)

Joe seems like the "nicest guy," but he becomes a maniac when he gets behind the wheel of his car. He's like Jekyll and Hyde. Everyone comments that he is "so easygoing" and "never gets angry," yet when he's driving home from work he screams at other drivers, honks his horn and sometimes threatens drivers who get in his way. Joe is calm on the outside and a "pressure cooker" on the inside. He internalizes the anger he feels at his bullying boss, and at home feels that his partner and children make so many demands on him that he can't possibly meet them adequately. He feels out of control everywhere in his life and "will, by God, be in control" in his own car.

Many like Joe experience work and home situations that generate frustration, anxiety and anger. People learn to suppress anger in relationships with friends and loved ones, fearing that if they express their anger they will be abandoned or hurt, or may hurt another. They don't express their frustration and anger at work for fear of losing their jobs. As day-to-day frustrations increase, suppression of anger can lead to the aggressiveness and the random violence we are observing on roadways, airways, stores, schools and workplaces when vulnerability and powerlessness are triggered. Anger that is repressed finds its outlet in anonymous bursts of rage toward total strangers.

Powerlessness and Vulnerability

Many individuals appear to be angry most of the time. They rage, bully and hurt others, become apologetic and contrite only to become enraged again the next time they feel out of control, vulnerable and powerless.

Arthur grew up in a family and community that shamed him for expressing sadness, fear or vulnerability. He was expected to be "tough" all the time and would be teased and hit if he showed any signs of weakness. Anger and rage were acceptable; tears, fears and powerlessness were not. Today when Arthur's child is sick, his wife cries, he faces layoffs at work, the family dog is injured, he loses a game, or any other time his feelings of vulnerability or powerlessness are triggered, he bypasses the real feelings, masking them with rage. He explodes: yelling, screaming, bullying and intimidating anyone in his proximity, projecting onto others the powerlessness and vulnerability he blocks in himself.

It is important to separate the act from the actor. Arthur's abusive outbursts are definitely beyond the pale and completely unacceptable. Outside he is a tyrant; inside he feels insecure, powerless, vulnerable and out of control. In order for Arthur to get control of his outbursts, it will be necessary for him to allow himself to feel his feelings of fear, insecurity, powerless and vulnerability.

All of us are responsible for our behavior. When you're feeling angry, you can be in control of it; when you're enraged, it's always in control of you. Alcohol doesn't "make us do it," and neither do others in our lives. The freedom to swing our arms ends where another's self begins.

Anger-obics[SM]: Move Your Body, Shift Your Mind

This Guy's the Limit

Think of a situation that recently made you angry. Or imagine someone is saying something nasty to you. (If you have trouble thinking of something, see appendix C for ideas.)

Stand tall. Notice your feet connecting to the floor—feel its full support beneath your feet. Make sure your knees aren't locked. Imagine any tension flowing down your body and out the soles of your feet.

Imagine the person saying the hurtful or provocative statement, or making a statement that is none of his or her business.

Take a deep breath. Bring your right foot forward and your right hand and arm forward with your hand facing the imaginary person, in a kind of "stop" gesture while you say the word "no." Say "no" forcefully and allow the sound to come from your belly, not your throat.

Try this several times, experimenting with your voice, your gestures, etc. How does it feel to stop the offending person? Do you feel strong? Scared? Powerful? Uncomfortable? Write about your experience here.

_____

_____

_____

Walk on It

If rage is a problem for you, here's a safe way to express your anger. It may give you a chance to stand back a bit and achieve balance. And it's sure to make you laugh at some point.

On the bottom of your shoe, write down the incidents, people or events that anger you. Enjoy walking around on them all week. When you feel angry, just walk a bit more. Stomp, even. At the end of the week, think about the difference between walking on the words versus exploding at someone or something. Was it helpful to have an alternative to raging during certain events? Is it freeing to see how you can release your anger without hurting anyone?

The Golden Healing Light

This exercise can be used as a foundation for many of the other exercises. It uses the imagery of Golden Healing Light. If you feel more comfortable with other imagery you may replace it with Holy Spirit, white light, Great Spirit, etc.—whatever feels right for you.

1. Sit or stand comfortably, with your spine straight.
2. Choose to allow the Golden Healing Light to bring you peace and relaxation and to help you release worries and concerns.
3. Close your eyes.
4. Allow your breath to be relaxed and just notice yourself breathing in and out.
5. Breathe in: In your mind's eye, picture a large circle of Golden Healing Light forming in front of you.
6. Breathe out: See yourself step into that circle. Imagine that you are surrounded by Golden Healing Light.
7. As you breathe in, you take in this magical light.

8. As you breathe out, you let go of tension, worries, or negative thoughts.
9. Imagine this light traveling through your spine, from the crown of your head, down your spine to your tailbone, and back up again.
10. The light suffuses your inner organs: lungs, heart, stomach, etc.
11. Imagine the light in your bones and muscles, and in your extremities (arms, hands, legs, feet, toes).
12. Picture this Golden Healing Light in every cell of your body.
13. Allow yourself to feel a sense of peace and happiness as the Golden Healing Light touches every part of your body.

Remember that whenever you are feeling stressed or angry you can return to this relaxed state by taking some time alone, closing your eyes and visualizing the Golden Healing Light.

You may wish to write notes here about your experience.

_____

_____

_____

_____

_____

_____

Note: This exercise was developed by trainer and counselor Jeff McFarland and is used with his permission.

Home Sweet Home

To start this exercise, you may want to do the *Gratitude Attitude Meditation* to get to a state of calm, or just stand and take a few deep breaths down into your belly. You can sigh or make a sound as you breathe out.

Imagine your life as a house and anger as a room in that house. Draw a picture of the room that is anger. No need to make it artistic. What do you put in that room?

When you're done:

- Notice what you've put in the room.
- Is there anything missing from the room (a door to get in and out, or to close for privacy, a window to see out, a light)?
- Add the things that are missing to your drawing.
- How do you balance this picture?
- Is there anything else you'd like to add?
- What insights does your drawing provide?

MAD PAD

DEPRESSION IS RAGE SPREAD THIN.

—*Paul Tillich*

> ANGER IS A SIGNAL, AND ONE
> WORTH LISTENING TO.
>
> —*Harriet Lerner*
> The Dance of Anger

CHAPTER 4

BRIDGE OVER TROUBLED WATER: Feeling Vulnerable

In this chapter, we explore how vulnerabilities contribute to unhealthy anger expression. You will discover some of the mistakes we make when our anger communication is unclear. You'll learn how to put an end to blaming and complaining—your own and others. You will also gain an understanding of how aggressive behavior and bullying can be rooted in fear of failure. You'll see how incorrect assumptions can lead to unnecessary anger and how to avoid this pitfall.

THE BLAME GAME

When grief and pain are not acknowledged or expressed, blame is passed around like a hot potato, eventually sticking to the hands of the ones who are least likely to be able to throw it away. When we grow up in or live in shaming environments, we quickly learn that we must blame or be blamed. When surrounded by shame, we learn that to make a mistake is to *be* a mistake. There are few compromises, and little effort is placed on trying to find solutions to problems.

Righteous Rilla Was Never Wrong

Rilla was a champion at playing the "blame game." She simply was never wrong. Others in her life were always to blame for her moods, behaviors or actions. Everything from the simplest feedback at work to her children's attempts to state their own opinions to the slow and meticulous way her husband folded the laundry was viewed as a personal attack.

Throughout her life, Rilla had the best coaches. Her parents cared more about appearances than substance, and taught Rilla that the easiest course to perfection was to make all her mistakes the responsibility of someone, or something, else. They were always willing to accept her excuses: She couldn't work with a particular teacher; the lessons were not made clear to her; the dog ate her homework. Frequently her parents would complete an assignment so she would win the required A. Rilla grew up convinced that she was incapable of achievement on her own and equally convinced that it wasn't her fault. Mistakes, or even differences of opinion, seemed like pointing fingers taunting her for her inadequacy. She became an athlete capable of winning the gold in the "Blame Game."

The Rules of the Game

When playing the "Blame Game" we learn that we must:

- Shift the blame to something or someone else as quickly as possible in order to protect our self-worth.
- Attack or excuse in order not to lose face or power when we feel cornered or are asked to be accountable.
- Always view others as potentially dangerous to our sense of well-being.
- Look out for "number one."

- Never look for a solution, only a place to attach blame.
- Never own up to a mistake. (We score the most points if we are always right.)
- Always blame the members of another team for our own mistakes, limitations and behaviors when playing in teams.

Some basic strategies in the "Blame Game" include: "because," "he/she made me," "I care more than you," "they are against me," "I didn't know," "my behavior is out of my control" and "scapegoat." (Middelton-Moz, 1999)

Hostility and aggression are frequently required in this game in order to justify our position. These ploys can either be expressed or kept inside where they can grow and fester. Playing the game often releases years of pent-up anger and frustration. Today our workplaces, relationships and communities seem to be full of pointing fingers. It feels like we are playing "emotional hot potato" every hour of the day. Passing the blame to someone else in order to protect fragile egos from more emotional wounds appears to be an international pastime.

The Game You Win by Not Playing

When deciding whether to play the "blame game," participants should know that winning, in fact, means losing. By "winning" consider the things we lose: dignity, temper, self-control, relationships, fairness, connection, love, knowledge, peace and self-esteem. A real win in the game is a decision not to play. Individuals, families and communities all win when the game is put aside in favor of accepting personal responsibility and consequences for our own actions.

Faced with the negative consequences described, you might benefit from knowing some positive guidelines that will help you avoid beginning the game:

- Another's differences in actions or belief don't make you wrong any more than another's similarities make you right.
- Constructive feedback is a gift that helps us change and grow. Don't personalize it.
- Accept accountability for your actions. There is a difference between the act and the actor. Passing blame only increases shame, powerlessness and a sense of incompetence.
- Learn to focus on solutions rather than staying stuck in the problem.
- Understand that blaming and complaining often have roots in anger and feelings of powerlessness. Learn to make friends with healthy anger.
- Pay attention to your conversations with others. Have you talked about the same problem repeatedly without attempting to find solutions? Are others "attacking" you or simply stating an opinion?
- Set limits on the time you are willing to listen to others complain or blame. By continuing to listen, you are taking part in the game.
- If you are being blamed for another's behavior, beliefs or feelings, don't take the bait; otherwise, you'll be tempted to defend and then the game is on. Pointing fingers doesn't accomplish anything and usually results in hurt feelings for all concerned. If the blaming continues, suggest a break and remove yourself until the other person is willing to continue the discussion without blaming.
- Admit your own behavior or mistake. If you did something to offend another, say so and make amends. If you feel you did nothing wrong, don't take on responsibility for someone else's actions. You might say that you are willing to work toward a solution, but you are not willing to be blamed.

- Don't accept group blaming in silence. (Group blaming is when an individual or group of individuals blame others, assuming, by your presence, that you agree with them.)
- Mistakes offer an opportunity to learn. Many famous and successful people credit their mistakes with teaching them the biggest lessons.

FEAR OF FAILURE

Six-year-old Tony stared at the test paper in front of him, accusing him, telling him what he already knew about himself. He had told himself often enough, "You're stupid." Suddenly, he started teasing Mary, taunting Jose, throwing spit wads at Jimmy. Later on the playground, he tripped Leroy, and then began punching him when Leroy tried to stand up. He'd been called "a bully," "aggressive," "a behavior problem." Anything was better than being called "stupid."

Ann had been promoted. She was expected to do a job that she had never been trained to do yet was afraid to ask for training for fear of being "demoted." After her promotion, she felt like "a failure," and lived in fear of what would happen if her boss and coworkers found out that she was out of her depth. Those who worked with Ann found that she was becoming more and more difficult to work with. "Ann used to be so nice, so open to feedback, so willing to support others. Now, she's always defensive when she is given the simplest feedback. Since her promotion, it's like she thinks she's perfect or something. She thinks she's better than the rest of us. Who does she think she is anyway?"

Megan was very successful in her work but nothing was ever good enough. She consistently had the feeling that she was "fooling people," and that if they ever looked carefully they would know she was "an imposter." Nothing had ever been good enough for her parents, and now nothing was good enough for her. If she received nine compliments and one piece of constructive criticism, she would dwell on the criticism.

If she got ten compliments, she felt guilty for fooling people. Needless to say, she could never win, and depression was her constant companion.

Often aggressiveness and bullying behavior are masks for fear of failure. Many children, like Tony, who have learning-style differences in school, become labeled as behavior problems. Before Tony was helped to understand that he learned differently from some of the other kids and was in fact extremely intelligent, he would start fights with classmates whenever he had to take a test. After the teachers came to understand his learning style, began teaching him the way he could best learn, and gave him tests that reflected his knowledge, his aggressiveness stopped.

Some individuals raised with impossibly high standards, unrealistic goals and unreasonable expectations believe that they have to be "perfect" or more successful than others. At the same time, they feel that they are constantly failing because nothing is ever good enough. Mistakes are all right for others, but never were or will be for them.

Those "fire-breathing dragons" in our lives who throw the tennis racket down in the middle of a game, start a fight when they get too close to commitment, become defensive with feedback, or blame coworkers for their failures, may be covering for fears of failure at sports, intimacy or their jobs, or the fear that they will receive proof that they are not as intelligent as others.

MAKING ASSUMPTIONS ABOUT OTHERS

A group of friends had come together to celebrate Sid's new promotion at work. As Sid was describing his new job, Shankar, Sid's best friend, groaned. Sid, seeing the pain on Shankar's face and hearing his pained expression, immediately assumed that he was angry at him for "bragging" about his new position and jealous of his good fortune.

Sid ignored his friend for several weeks, as his anger continued to simmer. He didn't need a friend who was jealous of his success. Finally, Shankar confronted Sid on his obvious distance. "Sid, have I done something to make you angry? It feels like you have been ignoring me lately. Maybe I'm wrong. I'd like to know. If you're angry, I'd like to talk with you about it. Your friendship is important to me."

"Well," Sid said sarcastically. "I just didn't want to bore you with my excitement at my new promotion." Shankar was flabbergasted. He had no idea what his friend was angry about. He was happy about Sid's promotion, and felt that it was about time he was acknowledged for his skill and hard work. He said as much to Sid, whose expression changed from fuming to perplexed. "But when I told you my news, you just frowned and made disparaging noises." Shankar thought for a minute and then exclaimed, "I wasn't jealous, I was sick! I had terrible indigestion and gas that night."

We Often Talk to Ourselves, Not to Others

Sometimes when we have been hurt by others in the past or have grown up in shaming environments, we learn to protect ourselves from more pain by becoming hypersensitive to the words, gestures, actions, facial expressions and behaviors of others. We try to read the minds of others in order to fulfill their needs, or to defend or remove ourselves from their presence so that we can protect ourselves from their anger or from further shaming. We attempt to minimize the wounds to our already injured egos by guessing at the other's needs, wishes and feelings in order to fulfill them or to prepare ourselves for "fight" or "flight."

Sometimes the answers we give ourselves when attempting to read another's mind enrage us, even though the other hasn't had the opportunity to be part of the conversation we play out in our minds. Shankar wasn't jealous of Sid's success; in fact, he was feeling happy that his friend finally was rewarded for his hard work. Sid, in his attempt to protect himself, misjudged Shankar's stomach pains for jealousy and anger.

Check It Out

Two of the biggest roadblocks on the path to creating and maintaining healthy and fulfilling relationships and a supportive environment for healing injuries to self-esteem are mind-reading and passing judgment. Mind-reading is believing that you know what another is thinking or feeling without checking it out: "She's angry at me because I asked her to stop by the store." "He doesn't love me anymore." "He's angry that I got the promotion." Passing judgment is unfairly evaluating another's behavior, character, feelings or motives: "He's just being kind because he wants something." "She doesn't care about anyone but herself." "He's jealous of me." "He always wants to be number one." We sometimes convict others in our minds without giving them the benefit of due process. Both mind-reading and inaccurate judgments frequently intensify angry feelings. (Middelton-Moz, 2000)

Sid made an inaccurate judgment regarding Shankar's thoughts and beliefs. He could have ended a valuable friendship if Shankar hadn't finally checked out his feelings that Sid was angry and was ignoring him. Below is Sid's thought process and what would have happened if he had checked it out:

Mind-Reading	Judgment	Reality Check	Fair Assessment
Shankar's angry about my promotion.	Shankar's jealous of my promotion.	Shankar had a stomachache. He was in pain.	Shankar's happy about my promotion and thought I should have been promoted long ago.

Over the next week, keep track of the number of times that you catch yourself mind-reading and making unfair judgments about others, then check out each one. You can follow the outline on the previous page and enter your results and feelings in the *Mad Pad* section of this chapter.

Mind-reading and passing judgment escalate our own unhealthy anger, and can sometimes lead to the spiral of unhealthy anger between ourselves and others. It is important to add some reality to our unfair evaluations. Not to be crass, but sometimes gas is just gas.

Anger-obics^{SM}: Move Your Body, Shift Your Mind

Solar Power

For this next exercise, and any other visualizations in this book, you may wish to tape-record the words with proper pauses, so that you can do the visualization without referring back to the text. Other options include: have a friend read it to you while you visualize; write the steps on index cards that you can refer to as you go; or try it once while referring back to the text, and a second time from memory, as best you can.

1. Stand straight with your feet hip width apart, knees relaxed.
2. Feel the Earth below you, supporting you completely. If you are standing on the floor, just imagine the Earth below you.
3. Imagine a nourishing energy flowing from the Earth and into your body, feeding every cell.
4. Imagine that the energy forms into a ball and moves through the crown of your head and up into the sun.
5. Imagine the ball of energy being charged by the sun. The light of the energy becomes stronger and stronger until it is like a ball of fire. Feel this energy return to you, glowing and hot.
6. In the ball of energy is strong power—the power to stand tall, the power to create, the power to speak your truth, the power to know all you need to know, the power to create change in your life, in your town, in the universe!
7. Picture this power as it courses through your body again. Feel the power especially as it moves into any parts of your body that are calling to you at this time.
8. When you feel ready to stop, let the ball of energy return down through your legs and into the ground.
9. Give thanks.
10. Imagine that you can call upon this powerful energy the next time you are angry. It can help you choose a healthy way to act or speak out. It can help you change a situation for the better.

Questions:

a) What was the experience like?

_____

_____

_____

_____

b) Write about what you imagine it might be like to call upon and utilize this power energy next time you're angry. What would make the experience different from your usual anger experiences?

_____

_____

_____

_____

Solar Power II

Try the Solar Power I again. Follow steps 1 to 7. This time, after step 7, notice the ball of energy as it moves through every part of your body as you continue on with steps 8 to 13 on the next page. You may wish to try the exercise using all the steps below, or you may want to just try one or two today, another the next time, since each step takes you into one or several areas of your body. Whatever you decide, end with steps 14 to 16 each time.

8. Feel the energy move into your crown, eyes, ears, nose and mouth. How does it feel in each of these places?

9. Can you experience the energy in your breath?

10. Feel the power energy in your throat. Is there a sound it wants to make? If so, go ahead and make this sound.

11. Feel the power in your shoulders, arms, hands. Do your hands and arms want to move in any way? If so, allow for the movement.

12. Feel the energy come back up into your torso, in your chest. How does it feel here? Are there any colors associated with the power in your chest? Any images?

13. Allow the energy to move to your solar plexus. What do you feel here? In your belly? Your genitals? Hips? Thighs? Knees? Calves? Feet? (Pause between each of these.)

14. When you feel ready to stop, let the ball of energy return down through your legs and into the ground.

15. Give thanks.

16. The next time something distresses you, remember that you can call upon this powerful energy the next time you are angry. It can help you choose a healthy way to act or speak out. It can help you change a situation for the better.

NOTE: Does the energy get stuck anywhere? If so, just notice where it's stuck. How does that stuck place look or feel? Does an image come to mind? If it does, allow the sun to come into the image and help you unblock that power energy.

Questions:

a) What was the experience like this time?

_____

_____

_____

_____

b) How did the power energy feel in the different parts of your body? You may wish to write any sensations, thoughts, emotions or images below. You may also wish to draw pictures next to some of them.

_____

_____

_____

_____

_____

Humor Me

You don't need to be an artist in order to produce cartoons. Just follow these simple steps and create your very own unique cartoon character. (Use a separate piece of paper so the cartoon can be as large or as small as you like.)

1. Take a deep breath, close your eyes and relax.
2. Imagine your angry self as a cartoon character. What comes to mind? Is the character a person of your gender, a different gender, an animal? Take a few minutes and just observe the character. Is his/her voice loud, soft, squeaky, grating? What does he/she look like?
3. Open your eyes and make a sketch of this character. It doesn't matter how well you draw—a stick figure is fine, too. Adding a distinct feature such as curly hair, glasses or body posture can give your cartoon figure "life."

4. Give your character a name.

5. Ask your character: "What do you believe is the best thing about getting angry?" or "Tell me something about anger."

6. Listen to your character. What does he/she say? Does it surprise you?

7. Write your character's response above his/her head. Circle the words and draw a line from the words to the character. You've created a cartoon!

8. You can also do this exercise imagining your wise self or calm self instead of your angry self.

Duck Back

You can use this exercise when you feel someone is insulting you or trying to hurt you. For now, remember a situation where it felt like the person was trying to hurt you with their words. If you can't think of a situation, just imagine someone insulting you.

Close your eyes. Take a few deep breaths into your belly; as you breathe out, imagine tension in your body releasing through your breath. Imagine the person's hurtful words are drops of water while you picture yourself as a duck. In your mind's eye, see the drops of water roll off your back. Try to feel the water dripping right off you. How does it feel to have the water/words roll off you without affecting you? Remember, you can also swim to another part of the pond, perhaps one where the rain is sweeter or the overhanging trees protect you. When the image feels complete, open your eyes.

You may wish to draw a picture of this image, including the insulting word. In the midst of "battle" you can use this or similar imagery, such as that of holding an umbrella.

Note: "Duck Back" was developed by trainer and counselor Jeff McFarland and is shared with his permission.

Safety Plan

Do you feel angry because someone is threatening your safety, making you feel powerless and vulnerable? For example, has someone said he or she will hurt you? Or has the person physically harmed you? If so, make a safety plan; that is, work out what you will do to make yourself safe. It is not okay to continue to be in an unsafe situation.

How is your safety being threatened?

_____

_____

What do you need to feel/be safe?

_____

_____

How could you make yourself safe? (For example, leave my partner; get a new job; get a restraining order against _____.)

_____

_____

What's stopping you from creating safety?

_____

_____

Who can help you get safety? (For example, friend, relative, acquaintance, lawyer, police, judge, crisis hotline, etc.)

_____

_____

CHAPTER 5

LET'S GET PHYSICAL:
Anger in Your Body

Much of our experience of anger is a physical one. In this chapter, we explore how anger affects our bodies, and how our bodies affect anger:

- Chemical and physiological changes take place in our body when we are angry.
- Ignoring the body's need for food, sleep or comfort can set off anger.
- Ingesting certain foods and other substances can affect anger.
- Pain and disease often trigger anger.
- Chronic anger can lead to pain and disease.

ANGER AS A PHYSICAL EXPERIENCE

The Present Tense

Most people tense up, tighten and constrict their bodies in some way when they are angry. Just as people with different personalities have varied ways of expressing anger, each of us has specific physical responses to anger, as well:

- Carole feels tired.
- Christoph experiences a backache.
- Stephan turns red in the face.
- Ming's throat and belly tighten.
- Carl becomes constipated.
- Wenlin gets a headache.
- Hina paces.
- Latoya clenches her jaw.
- Jon grinds his teeth.

Think about your own body. How do you experience anger? If you're one of those people who finds it hard to recognize anger, some of these body symptoms may provide a helpful hint. The *Anger-obics*^{SM} exercise, "Body Language," in this chapter can be especially useful to you.

Tension often goes hand in hand with anger, whether you fight against the anger and push it down, or express the anger verbally or physically. You may feel a rush of adrenaline and a sense of relief by releasing tension through hitting or screaming. The relief doesn't make yelling or hitting healthy. Research on anger shows that both holding anger in and forcing it out can be bad for your health.

The Dis-Comfort Zone

Often anger can feel terribly uncomfortable. Sometimes feeling angry is like having on a wet bathing suit full of sand, or sitting on a hot, sticky vinyl car seat for twelve hours: You just want to get out of your misery. When we're stuck in anger we are often focused on the mental qualities of anger, as if we are stuck in our own heads:

- We may continue to replay an upsetting situation in our minds without transforming it.
- We can remain mired in an old belief system. (For example, "Everyone's out to hurt me.")
- Our anger may remain unacknowledged, unexplored and/or unexpressed.

To resolve the anger, we need to be fully present in the moment, paying attention to our thoughts, our emotions and our bodies. As we do this, we may feel that wet, sand-filled bathing suit drying off: What a relief! Begin to explore the anger in your own body:

- Where do you hold your anger?
- Have you ever experienced the anger flowing out of your body?
- How does it feel when you finally let the anger go? Do your shoulders relax? Does your stomach calm down? What else happens?

You may want to note these answers on your *Mad Pad*.

Try watching someone practice tai chi or karate. The martial artist allows his or her body to fully relax. The energy and movements seem to flow effortlessly and effectively—blocking a kick, knocking the opponent off balance. As we work with the energy of anger in the body, through *Anger-obics*SM exercises and other means, we can learn to be relaxed and effortless like the martial artist. We can relax into the sensations and allow the energy to flow in a healthy way. As we do this, we see how anger informs us, what messages the anger brings. Then we can act upon the anger in an effective, positive way, without hurting ourselves or others.

WHEN YOU'RE HUNGRY, LONELY, SICK OR TIRED

The Big Mac™ Attack

Elsa felt her anger rise in her throat. She drove faster and cursed the slow drivers on the road. She yelled at her four-year-old son, Benny, to stop singing. Everything seemed to set her on edge. What was with the world? If Benny hadn't been in the car with her, she would have screamed at the top of her lungs. She passed a McDonald's™ and wished she hadn't just started her diet. "I sure could go for a burger and fries right now."

She turned sharply to avoid hitting a car. As she swerved, the organic fat-free cherry yogurt container flew off the seat, reminding her to eat lunch. She pulled into a parking space, gobbled up the yogurt and shared a few spoonfuls with Benny. Once her needs were taken care of and her belly was full, she felt much better. The anger served as a reminder to eat lunch!

The Big "Duh"

It's sometimes hard to remember that when we're tired, hungry or feeling sick, it's easy to feel angry. Perhaps we're angry at ourselves or others for not meeting our basic needs, or it may just be a physiological reaction. But the solution is simple—eat, sleep, take care of yourself.

In our hurry-scurry world, all dressed up and too many places to go, we often miss the signs of fatigue. Similarly, our thin-obsessed, fast-paced culture makes skipping meals and under-eating common. These can be steps on the road to ill health. In this case, anger can be an early warning system to change your habits. Sometimes anger carries a simple message: your body needs something!

Our friend Cindy recalls, "I still remember the day I realized that those angry, edgy feelings meant I needed a glass of water. I couldn't believe the solution was so simple—at least that time!"

Lonely Hearts, Tired Toes and Sorry Spleens

Your anger may also be a message that you need more love in your life: Touch, companionship and support are all human needs. Many of us are literally touch-starved. This doesn't mean you need to find a romantic partner in the next twenty-four hours. You can get a massage, make dinner plans with a friend, play with a friend's dog or cat, or ask your sister for a hug.

We're often so busy, we find it impossible to stop and discover what we need. Our bodies possess several means of telling us to slow down. The obvious way of getting this message across is fatigue. If we really overdo it, we get sick. But somewhere in between just plain tired and sick, there is often a stage of anger.

Many people become crabby when they haven't had enough sleep. Fortunately, the solution is an easy one: Sleep. You may find you need to be more regular in your patterns (go to sleep at the same time each night and get up at the same time in the morning), wake without using an alarm, use an alarm that wakes you gently, or even take a nap during the day. If you find it hard to fall asleep at night, try to uncover the cause: lack of physical exercise; caffeine, alcohol or sweets too close to bedtime; unresolved anxieties, etc.

If you are taking care of yourself, but pain or illness are still contributing to anger, perhaps you just need to acknowledge your anger and allow yourself to feel angry without dwelling on it excessively. Talking to a friend about it or doing one of our *Anger-obics*^{SM} exercises may help here.

Physical exercise can also be an important tool for transforming anger. Exercise releases endorphins, which help you feel good. Aerobic exercise changes the body chemistry of depression and can work as a natural antidepressant for some individuals. According to many ancient health philosophies, such as traditional Chinese medicine and Indian ayurvedic medicine, lack of exercise can cause stress, toxins and anger to build in the body. Exercise can discharge this negative or "stuck" energy, freeing up your vital "life force" energy.

CONSUMPTION, CHEMISTRY AND BODY CYCLES

Claudette recalls, "In my fifty years as a social worker, I really lost my cool a few times in the office—I was way out of line. Every time I'd had more than three cups of coffee." Just as anger affects your body, chemicals in your body can affect your emotions:

- Tak experiences a sugar meltdown after eating too many sweets. He finds himself becoming irritable at his kids and wife.
- Fifteen-year-old Keisha fights constantly with her mom and her brother the day before her period.
- Josh finds himself in an angry tirade whenever he drinks more than four beers.

Consuming sugar or drugs can trigger anger. In addition, some people drink alcohol in order to allow their anger to be expressed, since alcohol reduces inhibitions. In this case, the alcohol can serve as a permission slip to "blow up" or become violent. Hormonal changes, as occur in PMS, pregnancy, postpartum depression and menopause, can stimulate anger and other emotions. While less is known about men's hormonal cycles, it is quite possible that men's cycles affect their emotions, too.

Sweet Temptation

Holly's boss was a real jerk in the staff meeting—asking all kinds of questions to make Holly look bad. After the meeting, Holly visited the vending machine and scarfed down two Nutty Nougat bars. Later, her sister called to cancel their dinner plans because her new boyfriend was coming over. Another trip to the vending machine. This time it's a Chocomania bar. When Holly got home, she followed her Lean-and-Mean Vegetarian Lasagna with an entire quart of chocolate-chip ice cream. An hour later she felt bloated, depressed and angry at herself for overeating again.

Stuff It

Plenty of people eat their way through anger. Stuffing down food can be like stuffing down feelings. For some, eating can become a way to try to satisfy inner needs. If you're not taking care of yourself by acting upon the situation that makes you angry, "comfort food" can sort of, kind of, maybe, feel like nurturing yourself. Okay, it's not exactly nurturing, but it does make you feel temporarily better. Well, not exactly better, but different.

Sugar, chocolate, wine, beer, caffeine, cigarettes—all these substances alter your chemistry. Chocolate even contains a natural antidepressant, which your body might crave when you feel depressed. While these substances can change your emotional state, they are not a way of taking care of yourself. Their negative side effects can include weight gain, depression, disease and addiction. While we are not necessarily advocating abstinence, consider moderating your intake.

Puff, the Toxic Dragon

Jan's irritation seemed to grow throughout the day as she and her partner Brenda varnished the kitchen and living room floors. Everything Brenda did seemed to get on Jan's nerves. Brenda breathed too loudly, spoke too quickly and chewed too noisily. Jan also noticed that she'd been getting a headache and stuffy nose all day. At Brenda's urging, and despite her own resistance, she finally agreed to a walk outside. "Wow, I didn't realize how bad that polyurethane smelled until we got out here," said Brenda.

To Jan's surprise, after ten minutes her nose and headache symptoms disappeared, along with her anger. When she returned to the house, she experienced angry feelings within a few minutes. Some people report that chemical sensitivities turn on their "anger circuits." With accounts of chemical sensitivities on the rise, it is important to pay attention to this potential source of anger. While polyurethane may not be a problem for you, perhaps there are other substances lurking around your home or office affecting your health and emotions. Sensitivities can include foods, cleaning products, artificial colors, perfumes, dyes, additives, mold, fumes, furniture, paints, pesticides and other chemicals.

When our bodies are reacting to certain foods, drinks or chemical fumes, the anger is part of our body's healthy response. Perhaps it is the body's way of saying, "I don't like this. It isn't healthy for me." The good news is, when we change our unhealthy habit or toxic environment, this type of anger goes away.

HOW UNHEALTHY ANGER AFFECTS YOUR BODY

The Miracle of You

The human body is miraculous. Even tonsils, once thought useless, have an important function in preventing disease. Similarly, our body's response to anger makes sense once we understand nature's design.

The emotion of anger in itself does not harm the body. It's the tension (the way we hold anger) and continued stress of long-term, unhealthy anger that tends to cause the negative effects. Here's what happens in the short run:

- The adrenal glands, located just above your kidneys, pump extra epinephrine (adrenaline) and cortisol into your blood.
- Adrenaline pounds the heart muscle, forcing it to pump blood faster and raising blood pressure.
- The sympathetic nerves squeeze tightly, limiting blood supply to the kidneys, liver, intestines, stomach and skin, while adrenaline pumps the newly released blood supply to the lungs and muscles.
- Fats and sugars (glucose) in the blood increase, and blood pressure rises even higher.
- The blood supply to major organs decreases. (Middelton-Moz, 1999)

In prolonged stress response, many hormones are secreted, including: epinephrine and norepinephrine; ACTH and TSH (which stimulate other endocrine glands); cortisol, aldosterone and thyroxine (which stimulate certain organs such as the liver, kidneys and heart). (Schiraldi, 2002)

Fight or Flight or Just Plain Tight?

When we look closely, we understand that, in many situations, this physiological response, traditionally called fight or flight, protects us. If you were being chased by a wild boar or cornered by a dangerous thug, the above effects would help you run away fast or stay and fight. The body's energy would be used where most necessary (arms for fighting, legs for running), rather than where it's not needed (digestive system, immune system, etc.).

If you're like most people, neither a wild boar on your tail nor a back alley slugfest is a common occurrence—thank goodness! In this case, your body responds as if you are in danger, yet you do not run away or physically fight. When this happens frequently, whether you express your anger or not, you are stressing your body. In fact, such stresses can lead to disease.

Over time chronic stress or anger can:

- Thicken the heart-muscle tissue
- Force the heart to pump harder
- Thicken the artery walls
- Cause hyperventilation
- Weaken the immune system (by slowing the action of white blood cells and impacting the thymus gland)

When the body has been exposed to prolonged stress, it's as if the nervous system is in a state of alert, all the more ready to repeat the stress cycle again.

The Big Picture

What happens in the long run? Chronic unhealthy anger can contribute to headaches, back pain, decreased immunity, hypertension, ulcers, digestive problems, ulcerative colitis and heart disease. Unexpressed anger has its health costs, too. Several studies have linked suppressed anger to increased incidences of cancer and higher death rates from cancer. Studies of traditional Korean women who suppressed their anger show that suppressed anger can also affect the liver, gallbladder, lungs, spleen, kidneys, digestive system or heart. (Kang, 1981); (Lee, 1967); (Pang, 1990)

The Heart of the Matter

There is a research center in Boulder Creek, California, devoted entirely to scientific studies of the heart. Research done at the Institute of HeartMath gives us greater insight into the anger–heart connection and its role in health, performance and learning. These studies have shown that:

- When people experience joy, appreciation, love, compassion and other "positive" feelings, their heart rhythms reflect that their internal systems are in a more ordered state. In an ordered or coherent state, the immune system, nervous system, respiratory system and other body systems function effectively and efficiently.
- When people experience anger, their heart rhythms are in a state of disorder or incoherence. Frequent stress and incoherence can lead to disease.

While the HeartMath researchers do not advocate repressing anger, which can contribute to heart disease over time, they do recommend methods that use the heart's "intelligence," what many call intuition, to find a healthy solution to whatever problem is causing the anger. For instance, if you are often angry when waiting in line, you can use techniques to access your heart's wisdom and come up with a better response. These techniques may provide an internal feeling such as calmness, or they may provide a very specific solution you hadn't thought of, such as shopping in off-hours or bringing along a magazine to read while you wait. Whether you receive a concrete answer, a sense or a feeling, your body's unhealthy response (incoherent heart rhythm, respiration, blood pressure, etc.) is likely to shift to a more healthy and coherent balance. (Childre, Martin, Beech, 1999)

Body-Wise

The more you consult your body, including your heart, the more you will learn about your anger and how to live with it constructively. The body's wisdom is a great resource for a healthier, happier life. This doesn't necessarily mean getting rid of anger altogether. Anger has its positive role in alerting you to danger, threats and boundary violations. Accessing your body's wisdom means:

- Taking care of your body, including your physical, emotional and spiritual needs.
- Paying attention to tension, fatigue and cravings—signs that things aren't right—before you blow up or get sick from anger.
- Finding a constructive solution to your body's cues.
- Accessing your intuition, heart and all that your body knows to address anger.

Anger-obics^{SM}: Move your Body, Shift Your Mind

Body Language

1. Think of something that made you angry recently.
2. Replay the scene in your mind, remembering all the details you can.
3. As you think about the experience, try to notice how your body is feeling now, just thinking about the past situation. Are you more aware of any particular part of your body? Do you notice tension anywhere in your body? Where?
4. In the drawing on the next page, shade in the areas where you experience body tension, pain or other sensations. If you prefer, you may draw your own body outline and shade that in. Use a crayon or colored pencil to do the shading. You may wish to use different colors for tension, pain and other sensations. (Middelton-Moz, 2000)
5. Now that you have a sense where the anger resides, try one of these tools:
   - Focus on relaxing that part of the body next time you feel angry. You can do this by first tensing and then releasing the tension in that place.
   - Imagine breathing into that part of the body. With each exhalation, imagine yourself getting more in touch with whatever information you hold in your body. What is the pain/anger trying to tell you?
   - Go back to your drawing and allow a word to emerge. Write it down by the drawing. Does that word provide any insight into how you carry or express your anger?
   - Focus on one of the places where you experience pain. Try the Gratitude Attitude or Golden Healing Light, or another technique for relaxing; then focus on this part of your body and ask if it has any message for you—a word or phrase to give you insight. If you have trouble getting an answer, try breathing while focusing on your heart; as you focus on your heart, ask for an answer.

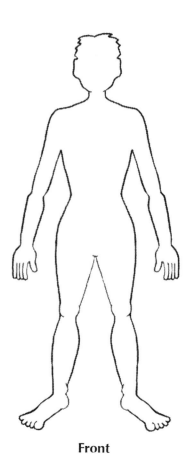

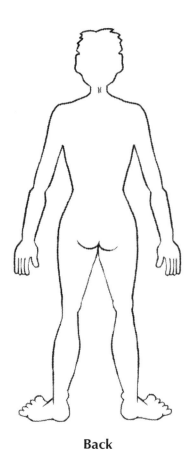

Front   **Back**

Salome's Silky Scarf Dance

Find a large silk scarf or piece of light fabric. If you have the luxury of choosing, pick one that has a color that makes you think of anger. Hold the scarf in your nondominant hand (left if you are a rightie, right if you are a leftie). If you want, you can put on some "stormy" music, classical or whatever type you prefer.

Imagine that the scarf personifies your anger, and you are witnessing it without judgment. Allow the scarf to move in your hand as you move or dance with your anger. Does the scarf cover your face in the beginning? Does it wave madly up and down? Does it wrap itself around your body? As you move, do you find it changing? Does it become quieter or wilder?

You don't need to interpret with your mind. Just allow the movement to take place without judgment or ideas about what it means. Write any notes here or draw a picture of the scarf mid-dance and give it a title. Did the exercise provide any insights into your anger?

Map the Pain

Draw an outline of your body below. Be a detective: During the next week, shade in the areas on your drawing where you experience body pain. Use a crayon or colored pencil to do the shading. After you have identified the areas of pain or numbing, write what you were doing, feeling or expressing before the pain began. Also write down who was with you. (Middelton-Moz, 2000).

Clay-by-Clay

This exercise employs clay. However, if you don't have clay, you can do the whole exercise just imagining the hunk of clay. Alternatively, you can make your own "clay-dough" using the recipe below.*

Take several deep breaths, breathing into your belly. Remember what it feels like to feel angry. You might think of a time recently when you felt angry or use a situation from appendix C. Where in your body do you imagine the anger resides? Imagine reaching into that part of your body and taking out a chunk of clay that represents the anger.

As you hold the real or imaginary clay in one hand, what movements does your other hand wish to make with the anger/clay? Allow yourself time to play with the anger/clay. Do the movements change over time? How does that relate to your expression of anger? Now use the other hand to work with the anger/clay. Does this hand respond differently to the anger/clay? Now use both hands to work the clay. What movements are you making with two hands? Do these movements provide any insights into your approach to anger?

Write about your experience below.

---

*Dough recipe from *Mudwork: Creative Clay, Dough, and Modeling Experiences* (Kohl, 1989): Combine 4 cups flour, 1 cup iodized salt and 1¾ cups warm water in a bowl. Knead for ten minutes. It's ready to use.

MAD PAD

THE HATRED YOU'RE CARRYING IS A
LIVE COAL IN YOUR HEART—FAR MORE
DAMAGING TO YOURSELF THAN TO THEM.

—*Lawna Blackwell*
The Dowry of Miss Lydia Clark

WE BOIL AT DIFFERENT DEGREES.

—*Ralph Waldo Emerson*

CHAPTER 6

GETTING TO KNOW YOU:
Anger and Couples

In this chapter, we explore the role of conflict in intimate relationships: how past history can play into a present relationship and how to cultivate a healthy relationship. You will find out how to change destructive patterns. You will learn tools and strategies for expressing anger in ways that support a strong and satisfying relationship with your partner.

THE PEAKS AND VALLEYS OF INTIMACY

Sally and Greg's relationship is one of respect and mutual support. In their sixties, they love to play tennis and hike. Yet the two are very different people. Sally has written and posted detailed instructions on how to load the dishwasher. Greg lives for spontaneity and a bit of chaos. He likes to take off skiing at a moment's notice.

Greg compares their relationship to an effective football team: "The quarterback's skills are different from the linebacker's, but you need both to score points." Greg accepts that Sally's posted instructions and detailed "to-do" lists are symbolic of her skill at organizing the household. Sally realizes that Greg's fun-loving nature and spontaneity are part of what makes the family fun, making it easier for her to tolerate his sudden ski trips. Their arguments tend to stay focused on the specific issue at hand and do not spill over into criticism of each other's personality traits.

It wasn't always like this. Greg admits, "Early on in our marriage, we both thought about divorce. We were so angry at each other. I guess what kept us together was that we came from broken families where divorce had hurt everybody. We didn't want that."

The Road Not Taken

It's important to remember that conflict in a relationship actually demonstrates that partners care and that they trust each other enough to face those conflicts. Successful conflict builds trust that leads to true intimacy and love. Most couples face challenges in their relationships. Relationships are filled with peaks and valleys. Often we view the peaks as the end-all and be-all. But while the valley may not have the breathtaking views of the mountaintop, it does have its own gifts: wildflowers, a sparkling brook and wild strawberries to taste and savor.

If you think of the very first mountaintop as the peak of infatuation and lust, you can probably remember a time that first valley seemed like such a disappointment. What a shock to discover you were traversing the mountain with someone who chews cereal loudly enough to wake up the neighboring campers. This progression out of initial infatuation may take you by surprise.

However, those couples who never fight, who never enter the valley, are at the most risk for eventual separation. We are surprised when the "perfect couple" separates because "they never argued." Exactly. Conflict, successfully dealt with, builds the trust that is necessary for real love. And that is why time in the valley is so important.

Time in the valley can mean fighting about dirty dishes in the sink, coping with different communication styles, noticing little pet peeves or feeling uncomfortable with intimacy. Time in the valley means seeing the person for who he or she really is—not just the projection you fell head-over-heels for in the beginning. Often, people get the urge to exit the relationship when they enter the valley. For some, exiting means leaving the relationship; for others it is workaholism or emotional distance. These couples are missing one of the very first treats of the valley: the wildflowers.

As conflict comes up in a relationship, the wildflowers can be seen as the little (and big) things we learn about one another through conflict: each other's frailties, as well as strengths. If we approach our anger with care, it can open up a new world enabling us to stretch our comfort zones and grow. The sparkling brook may be the time you spend holding each other after successfully negotiating the troubled waters of your first real fight—ah, trust! And the wild strawberries may be the increased intimacy you experience over time: It takes work, but there's nothing like that taste! Once we traverse the valley, the next peak can be higher, offering an even more amazing view than the first.

ACKNOWLEDGING THE PATTERNS OF THE PAST

The Ties That Bind

Often, our relationship with our parents (a manipulative mom, an emotionally distant dad, a finicky grandfather or grumpy grandma) resurfaces in marriage or other intimate relationships. We reenact our first love relationships because that is where we learned what love is. Our parents gave us our definition of love that shaped our beliefs. We project onto our partner how we felt as a child in conflict with our parents. It's as if we are talking to our parent when we say to a mate:

- "You don't love me."
- "You're always trying to control me."
- "You're so overbearing."

If your reaction seems extreme for the particular situation, it is likely that past relationships and experiences are being triggered.

*You are your **last ten** relationships.* Whatever unfinished business hangs on from a past liaison is brought into the present—jealousy, emotional abuse, resentment concerning an affair or any other issues that surfaced in the past—will haunt the present unless you address and heal them.

Another unhealthy dynamic is that sometimes we are attracted to the very qualities in another person that we don't allow for in ourselves. Then we despise the person for it or seek to control it in him or her for the rest of the relationship. For example, if we don't let ourselves cry, we may get triggered and become angry when our lover cries. Examining our past can shed light and help us accept such qualities in our partner and ourselves.

Here are some questions to help you begin to unravel the knots of your childhood and past relationships:

- From whom did you learn how to be angry?
- What hurtful actions did your parents take that trigger angry emotions in the present?
- How do those role models handle conflict?
- How do past romantic relationships shape your current beliefs about anger?
- As an adult in the present, do you expect your partner to satisfy unmet needs, such as recognition, security and worthiness? How can you also take care of yourself?

Once you understand your own motivations and triggers, you can begin to try to understand those of your partner. If you can feel some compassion for your partner and know that he/she is coming from a "hard place" emotionally, it can take the edge off some of your interactions.

Sally may still wish Greg was less spontaneous, but knowing he is responding to feelings of being powerless as a child reminds her that his behavior is not about her. Similarly, Greg can tell himself that Sally's notes are a response to the out-of-control feeling she had growing up with a father who was often intoxicated and unpredictable.

CULTIVATING A VIBRANT RELATIONSHIP

How Green Is Your Valley?

You need the right environment to nurture a relationship and help it grow. Just as you cannot grow petunias in the desert, you cannot deal with conflict constructively if your relationship is arid. Look at the environment in which your relationship takes place: Are you kind to one another? Do you hurt each other often? Do you do special things for each other? Let little annoyances ride? Speak kindly? Say "thanks"?

Stephen Covey compares a relationship's strengths and stressors to a bank account. If your balance is low, a check can bounce; your account becomes overdrawn. In relationships, we need to make deposits into our partner's account. Otherwise the balance will get low and little things will throw the account into negative territory. Then we will fight about little things—the bed is not made properly; there is not enough gas in the car; the dishes sat too long in the sink; and on and on. (Covey, 1989)

You can make deposits by kind words, hugs, helping out when not expected, a kind note on the refrigerator door, gifts or dinner out together. Here is a secret: Different people like to be loved in different ways. Ask your partner, "What makes you feel loved?" For some people, it is a clean living room; for others, it is a loving word or an arm around them while they cook dinner.

When they were first married, Greg felt helpless when Sally cried. Later she told him, "I come with an instruction manual. When I cry, you don't need to say anything or fix the problem. Just hold me."

External forces also affect the relationship environment. Are your jobs satisfying, demanding or horrific? Are finances strong or stressful? Are you both in good physical health? If you are feeling resentful for putting things into the partnership, then it may be a sign you need to fill up your tank somewhere. You may find that exercise, a spiritual practice, nurturing friendships, women's or men's groups, or an engaging hobby can be helpful.

If something outside of the relationship is causing anger or stress, try not to take your anger out on your partner. People often project anger onto loved ones, because it may seem to be the safest place. Try to explore honestly where your anger is truly stemming from. Use your own exploration, or ask a friend or counselor for help. Then try to communicate honestly with your partner: "I'm really angry that my boss changed the deadline on this project. I'm not sure I can finish it in time and I feel like I'm ready to lose my cool at the least provocation."

The Rage Circuit

Recent research on the brain shows that there are seven primal networks, one of which is unhealthy anger. The body responds to each particular situation by releasing certain neurohormones that trigger one of these seven mood circuits. So depending on the situation, our body has a patterned way of dealing with similar situations and will tend to trigger a particular mood. Once we are in a state, it's difficult for the brain to change to another neuroemotional state. (Atkinson, 2002)

Therapist Brent Atkinson utilizes this research in his framework for helping couples strengthen those emotional circuits that create intimacy so that they are able to trigger a positive mood rather than unhealthy anger. To trigger a partner's nurturing circuitry, Atkinson teaches couples to essentially issue a plea for help. A plea for help in one partner can naturally stimulate a nurturing response in the other. As Atkinson points out, neuroemotional brain research suggests that "each time neurons fire in a new pattern, pathways get strengthened as though new emotional grooves are being dug in the brain." (Atkinson, 2002)

Essentially, the more we exercise the new patterns, the easier it becomes. In the beginning, developing new patterns can be especially challenging:

- Do you know how to activate your partner's nurturing response?
- Does he/she know how to activate yours?
- Are there ways you could allow yourselves to be more vulnerable? Ask for help? Honestly tell each other that you feel hurt? Scared? Stressed?

At one point in their relationship Sally and Greg found themselves in a fight on Saturday mornings. Sometimes Sally fumed over Greg's newspapers scattered about the kitchen table. Other mornings Greg led the fight over how they would spend their day. Their therapist pointed out that Saturday morning is the most common time for couples to fight.

In a sense, the fight is a point of reentry. After a busy week with modest interaction, the conflict is a way to reestablish connection. Once they understood this, Sally and Greg were able to catch themselves and find other ways to reconnect after a busy week. They decided to begin their Saturday mornings with a brief check-in. Each shared how they were feeling that morning and what they felt they needed most. Without knowing it, they were employing the very techniques that Atkinson teaches, activating each other's nurturing response.

HANDLING CONFLICT IN HEALTHY WAYS

What Do You Fight About?

There are two reasons to argue: one is to let off steam and the other is to resolve issues. Many times we think we want resolution, but the way we fight actually insures that there will not be resolution. Rather than let off steam, our fight creates a pressure cooker where each issue raised just adds to the pressure in the pot.

Over time couples tend to push each other's buttons, all the things that drive us crazy:

- Household responsibilities/duties: *"Why am I always the one to empty the dishwasher?"*
- Money: *"You spent $500 on clothes?"*
- How to bring up their kids: *"You're too strict with them."*
- Emotional availability: *"You never want to talk."*
- Sex: In Woody Allen's film *Annie Hall*, Diane Keaton's character tells her therapist that they have sex *"all the time, at least once a week,"* while Woody Allen's character complains they *"hardly ever have sex, about once a week."*
- Workload/balance: *"You're never home."*
- Neatness or cleanliness: *"Have you forgotten how to use a clothes hanger?"*

If you find yourselves having the same arguments over and over, are you trying to change your partner to make him or her neater? More helpful? More emotionally present? What is lurking behind the fighting? Do you start fights in order to get closer to your partner? Frieda, a woman whose partner pushed her around, admitted, "For me, an angry touch is better than no touch at all." Or are you picking a fight to release stress? We all know our partners very well—enough to start a fight with them in two and a half seconds!

Examine How You Fight

Greg was a shouter. Sally was the silent-treatment type. She'd get her anger out in passive-aggressive ways, like saying something biting about Greg in front of his friends or implying Greg wasn't doing his share of the work around the house.

The most effective style in conflict resolution is to state the facts objectively, let your partner know your reaction to those facts, state what you need or want, and then listen to your partner to discover his/her perspective and needs.

What's your style? Do you run away from conflict? Do you push your anger down? Or do you get louder and louder as a fight goes on, heaping on larger insults as your stone-faced mate stares you down?

Experiment with your style. Choose one or two new strategies from the menu below and write them on your *Mad Pad* as a reminder. Try them in your next few arguments:

- **Take Two:** Taking a "time-out" can help you both regain perspective and fight from a "cooler" place, rather than fighting while your anger hormones are raging.
- **Watch Your Language:** Avoid blaming and hurtful words.
- **Don't Throw or Catch Hot Potatoes:** When a foul mood hits, you may be tempted to try to pass the anger and negativity off on someone else. You may get to pass it off this round, but it will return. Recognize when your partner throws a hot potato and bypass a fight by not engaging.
- **Admit Your Frailties:** Ask for forgiveness when you are wrong. "Please forgive me" can be the sweetest words to your partner's ears. The words may be hard to say, but they work like Miracle-Gro™ on the marriage tree.

- **Don't Interrupt:** If you find yourselves interrupting each other, use a timer. Take turns while each person talks uninterrupted for five minutes.
- **Shift the Pattern:** Try changing your behavior. For example, if you usually disagree with his/her points, try to agree. Walk down a different path to get different results.
- **Appreciation:** Acknowledge something positive about your partner.
- **Conscious Conflict:** You will find more strategies and a whole framework for resolving conflict in chapter 8.

The Heebie-Jeebies

You haven't had an unhealthy fight in three weeks. You feel more appreciated than ever before, and blossoms are blooming on the marriage tree. Does this new intimacy make you nervous? Maybe you're waiting for the other shoe to drop. Maybe yelling made you feel more powerful. Maybe you're a chaos junkie—to feel fully alive you need drama in your life, and fighting provided the drama. Ask yourself what you really want.

Sometimes people react to intimacy by growing numb. They find that old feelings of fear and helplessness come up and so they push their partners away in an effort not to feel. They may think they are falling out of love. They do whatever it takes to drive their partner away, but as soon as their partner becomes distant, they appear immensely desirable. We want them gone but fight to get them back. We call this dynamic "go away closer." Sometimes we push a loved one to see just how far we can go. "Will she still love me if I don't act lovable?" Neither of these is healthy behavior, and is probably rooted in ancient history. A therapist or counselor may be helpful as you work to explore and to change such behavior.

Many of us try to justify our own end of a disagreement. We think that if the other person just understood why we did what we did, they'd realize we're right. The problem with justifying is that it's only about "me." Try sharing the stage. If you find yourself trying to convince your partner of your motives and correctness, try this in your next fight: Stop justifying yourself for just a minute. Instead, attempt to hear what the person is saying. Rather than seeking to prove that you didn't mean to hurt him or her and explaining your actions, say, "I'm sorry that _____ hurt you." After your partner's hurt feelings have been acknowledged, he or she might be more willing to hear that a mistake is only a mistake.

For the Hot-Headed

If you tend to lose your temper easily, here's a simple exercise to cultivate patience:

- Next time you lose your temper, instead of focusing on your shame or who's to blame afterwards, take time to reimagine the situation. Recall how anger or resentment built up before the explosion. How could you have addressed your needs sooner, before the pressure intensified? Is there a way you could have acted without yelling at, blaming or hurting your partner? Could you have taken a time-out?
- Close your eyes and picture yourself in a similar situation in the future, doing everything right: monitoring your feelings, noticing when anger and resentment surface, and addressing your needs in a healthy way.

You may want to make notes about this on your *Mad Pad*.

Sometimes people are addicted to the hormone rushes of shouting, lashing out or expressing anger in other unhealthy ways. If you begin to wean yourself from the hostile response, you may find yourself feeling a bit bored. Such feelings of boredom are normal for a while.

And Remember This

Usually, what we take personally is not personal at all. You and your partner each react to behaviors that set something off in you. Your partner probably isn't trying to hurt you, and you're not trying to hurt him or her. You're both reacting to pain you carry from past experiences.

Resolving conflicts, sharing experiences and showing love for one another—emotionally, physically and sexually—keep people together. Where there are plenty of hugs, kisses, snuggles, compliments, shared pleasures and common activities, self-esteem grows. With this comes the joy of giving of yourself. In such a loving and healthy environment, you can express anger in a way that increases understanding and allows intimacy to flourish.

Anger-obics^{SM}: Move Your Body, Shift Your Mind

Changing the Game

Think of someone who tends to say things that hurt you, or think of a situation where you felt emotionally hurt or threatened. Write about that situation here:

_____

_____

_____

First, you will examine whether your beliefs and perceptions of the situation are correct:

1) Do you think the person intends to hurt or threaten you?
   ○ Yes   ○ No   ○ Maybe

2) Is this a person you can safely check out your beliefs with (can you trust him or her)? [If no, skip to step 5.]
   ○ Yes   ○ No   ○ Maybe

3) Imagine what it might be like to share your experience and ask the person what his or her intention is. What do you think he or she might say?

_____

_____

_____

4) If the person is likely to say he or she meant to hurt you, skip to step 5. If the person is likely to say he or she doesn't want to hurt you, do you think that's true or is he or she fooling him/herself?

_____

_____

_____

Now we will reframe the situation by changing your focus.

5) Imagine you are growing large like a giant and immune to being hurt, or imagine you are a spider on the wall, watching the situation from a neutral perspective. How does the situation look from here?

_____

_____

_____

From your new vantage point:

6) Is there a way to defuse the situation? Can you think of a way to derail the person's train from the direction it's going?

_____

_____

_____

7) If you want to take this exercise a step further, let your creativity loose for a minute, not worrying about whether you would really do this: Can you think of a truly outrageous but safe way to stop the person from saying something hurtful? Could you make a weird sound? Say something humorous or totally out of character? Dance on the kitchen table?

_____

_____

_____

8) Now have fun making up a story of how you respond to the situation. You can make your response serious, humorous or totally absurd!

_____

_____

_____

_____

_____

_____

_____

_____

_____

Stop 'til You Drop

This is an exercise that works best with a partner. However, you can imagine the partner if you prefer. This exercise is especially useful for someone who has trouble setting boundaries, particularly when his or her physical space is invaded. Read the exercise once through and then do it.

Tell the person ahead of time that when you say, "stop," they will need to stop moving toward you. Now have the person start out six feet away from you and slowly walk toward you. When it feels like the person gets too close to you for comfort, hold out your hand in a "stop" gesture, palm facing the person and fingers pointed to the sky. Say "stop" very clearly.

How does it feel to set a clear boundary? Write about any feelings that came up when you did this exercise, or draw a picture of you and your partner doing the exercise.

Domino Effect

Think of a time you yelled at a partner, spouse or child. Close your eyes and picture your angry response as a color, a jarring sound and/or a yucky feeling traveling from you to the other person. Imagine this color/sound/feeling blasting the other person and then traveling from them to other people, resounding across the planet. Truly, how we express our anger does affect our loved ones, which, in turn, can affect people we don't even know!

Now take a few breaths and focus on your heart. Picture a loving color and/or imagine or make a loving sound. Focus on the loving feelings in your heart. (If you have trouble feeling loving, use Gratitude Attitude or the Golden Healing Light meditation to help you come to a loving feeling.)

Picture yourself in the same situation with the person, but instead of sending him or her an angry color/sound/feeling, imagine sending that person the loving color/sound/feeling. Picture this loving color/sound/feeling traveling to him or her, and through that person, to many other people.

Bye Low, Cell Hi!

Biochemist Bruce Lipton, Ph.D., has integrated research from a variety of sources, including articles published by such respected journals as *Nature* and *Scientific American,* on the relationship between belief and health and how thoughts and beliefs affect the biochemical processes in the body. This research indicates that our negative or positive thoughts and beliefs can have a corresponding impact on the cellular level [see references for more information on the work of Dr. Lipton and his colleagues].

Write down some negative thoughts or beliefs you tell yourself. For example, "I can never get my needs met," "Everyone takes advantage of me," or "My mother always treats me like a child." Write a few positive thoughts you tell yourself. For example, "I'm good at _____," "I really enjoying doing _____," or "I like to spend time with _____."

On the next page are cartoon drawings of your brain cells. Pick one of your negative thoughts and write it in the first "balloon" or "caption" as if the brain cell is thinking that thought. Draw a picture next to the first cell of what your cartoon brain cell might look like after thinking the negative thought. (Drawing skills not necessary.) For example, it might change color, get bigger, become smaller, change shape, etc.

Pick a positive thought from your list. Write it in the balloon below the first one. Draw a picture of the brain cell reacting to this thought.

When you find yourself having negative thoughts, you may want to remember your image of the cell in positive thoughts. Close your eyes, breathe deeply and picture your image of the cell in positive thinking.

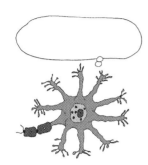

Cell with negative thought

Cell reacting to negative thought

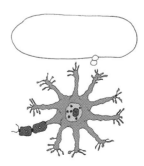

Cell with positive thought

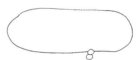

Cell reacting to positive thought

MAD PAD

YOU CANNOT SHAKE HANDS WITH
A CLENCHED FIST.
— *Indira Gandhi*

IF YOU JUDGE PEOPLE, YOU HAVE
NO TIME TO LOVE THEM.
                    — *Mother Teresa*

CHAPTER 7

HUSH LITTLE BABY:
Anger with Our Children

This chapter will help you identify and understand how and when a child's behavior triggers an unhealthy anger response. We offer problem-solving techniques and effective strategies for parents and others who take care of, or are involved with, children. You will also learn ways to help children deal with their own anger. The chapter ends with suggestions for helping children cope with bullying behavior and situations where they are frightened or intimidated by someone else's anger.

SEPARATING YOUR PAST FROM YOUR CHILDREN'S PRESENT

Waaaaaaaaaaahhhhhhhhhhhhhhhhhhh! It starts when they're babies. They cry. You try to feed them, put them to sleep, massage an aching belly. Nothing works. Their cries get louder. One hour, two hours, you're completely sleep-deprived and this little being seems inconsolable. You may feel helpless, angry, frustrated, sad or afraid. Sometimes you may even feel surprised to realize that instead of giving you love, this little bundle actually needs it. And the baby's cries seem to say, "Your love isn't enough." Eventually your patience runs out. You may yell at someone (partner, baby, other family member), cry or try to get away, if only for a few minutes.

A baby's (or child's) cry is a trigger for many parents. When they hear their children cry, parents' own past feelings of powerlessness can be triggered. On top of trying to meet the child's need, the parents must face uncomfortable feelings of their own. To model healthy behavior for your children, it is helpful to identify:

- Behaviors in your child that trigger you
- How you respond to those triggers
- How you can change your unhealthy responses
- The help you need in order to change your problematic behavior

When you're triggered, if you tell yourself that your child knows better and is just trying to provoke you, you're helping your anger escalate. *Boiling Point: The Workbook* identifies many triggers that lead to unhealthy parental anger. Which of these triggers apply to you? What messages do you give yourself when you're triggered? Note them on your *Mad Pad*.

- My child doesn't do what I tell her or him to do.
- My child won't stop crying.
- My child lies to me.
- My children fight.
- My children fight in the car and won't stop.
- My child won't share.
- My child won't eat something I've cooked.
- My child won't do assigned chores.
- My child misbehaves in stores.

- My child won't do his or her homework.
- My child talks back.
- My child leaves things lying around the house.
- My child keeps interrupting me when I'm talking on the phone.
- My child won't answer me when I'm asking a question.
- My child says she's already done something when she hasn't.
- My child takes things without asking.
- My child throws a tantrum over not getting his or her own way. (Middelton-Moz, 2000)

Most of the behaviors above are things that every child does. In fact, some are very healthy in certain developmental stages. If your two-year-old is saying "no," he's just doing his developmental job. It's nothing personal. Perhaps your child is asserting his independence, seeking your attention or testing boundaries. It's important to acknowledge the need behind the behavior, yet also set limits with your child and encourage respectful behavior. First, though, you need to calm down.

Note: Thanks to All That Matters in Wakefield, Rhode Island, for the fortune appearing in this cartoon.

RECOGNIZING CHILDREN'S DEVELOPMENTAL STAGES

Three-year-old Ruby loved going shopping with her mother. She loved pushing the little shopping cart the store provided and pretending to buy all the wonderful things she saw. When they stopped at the bakery counter for her mom to buy some bread, Ruby spied a pan of brownies. Heaven! "Bwownie! Bwownie! I want one!" she cried. "I know you'd like one," her mom replied, "but Mommy brought you a cookie from home." She reached in her bag and offered Ruby an oatmeal cookie. Ruby looked at the grainy cookie and then back at the luscious brownie. No comparison. "I want a BWOWNIE!" Ruby yelled, striking her mother's leg. Her mother calmly replied, "I understand that you feel frustrated, honey, but you can't have a brownie today and you can't hit." Eventually her mom's patient coaxing succeeded and Ruby enjoyed munching on the tasty cookie.

On the other side of the market, Danny and his mom were having a somewhat different experience. They had passed by the magazine rack and Danny had seen a Spiderman comic. "I want that!" he demanded. "You've got three at home," his mother said, "and I'm not buying you another." "I want THAT one!" Danny shouted, his face growing purple. "Stop that!" his mother hissed, "You're embarrassing me!" However, Danny, who was a veteran of such wars, persisted and finally his mother relented. "All RIGHT!" she fumed, slapping him on his butt. "Here's your comic. Enjoy it—you'll be in your room for the rest of the day. You're driving me crazy!"

Ruby is learning that she can have her frustrations and anger, but also must have internal limits on how she expresses them. She is also learning to tolerate disappointment and anxiety, and that she can't always get what she wants when she wants it. Danny is learning that bad behavior will eventually get him the thing he wants, but that there is a price to pay: isolation and punishment. He is learning anxious attachment. He still has yet to learn that at times he will need to delay his gratification.

Adolescents can seem to be returning to similar lessons as toddlers, but with a great deal more sophistication.

They are asking the questions: "Can I leave you without losing you?" "Can I be with you without losing me?" "Who am I anyway?" At this time they're integrating the lessons learned as a young child with the world of peers and their experience of the present. They are learning about their growing sexuality, and the difference between sex and nurturing. They struggle between independence and dependence as they face leaving home. They need support to safely explore their independence; at the same time they need firm limits when they stray onto unsafe ground.

Jules tells the story of his nephew, Aiden, who came to him distraught one day after his parents heard about his noisy partying with his friends in the town square. "Uncle Jules, why am I always in trouble?" Jules replied, "You're sixteen. It's your job to be in trouble. And it's your parents' job to find out when you are." Jules knew that Aiden's parents would provide appropriate limits for Aiden. He figured his role was to reassure Aiden that he'd outgrow his trouble stage.

STRATEGIES AND TECHNIQUES

Below are some helpful ways you can disengage from triggers sparked by your child—infant, toddler, youth or adolescent:

- Recognize when you're beyond mild frustration and that feelings from your past are being triggered in the present.
- Take a deep breath.
- Acknowledge the old powerless feelings, and soothe yourself with a message of, "I'm an adult now. This is the present. I am safe. I can handle this. I will do my best to help my baby/child."
- Give yourself a time out. Either make sure your child is safe and leave the room, or tell your child you're taking time out and sit down without talking for a few minutes.

- Tell yourself not to personalize it, and understand what is normal for your child's age or development.
- Do something physical: jumping jacks, dancing or a favorite *Anger-obics*ˢᴹ exercise!
- If you tend to hit, put your hands in your pockets or clasp them behind your back.
- If you're afraid that you're in danger of hurting your child, call 1-800-4ACHILD.
- Seek out the support of someone you trust to process feelings from the past. This will help you return to the present. It is important whenever possible to get support.

A few words about getting support: Years ago, most parents had help—it literally did take a village, or at least an extended family, to raise a child. Today, we don't often have these resources. Whether you're a parent, extended family member or caregiver, parenting without breaks leads to exhaustion, frustration and anger. Figure out what support you do have: trusted neighbors, friends or family can give you the time off you need to recharge before you lose your cool. Work time off into your weekly routine; don't wait for a crisis to hit. If you can't hire a baby-sitter, perhaps you can exchange childcare with another parent.

When you've taken some of the steps above, you are ready to address the specifics of the situation. Even in an urgent situation, one deep breath and taking time out can mean the difference between being ruled by the past or motivated by the present.

Wearing Your Child's Shoes

Okay, you can't wear your child's shoes, but you can pretend. Imagining what he/she is experiencing will help you find appropriate solutions. Once you have dealt with your triggers and calmed down a notch, ask yourself why your child may be acting the way he is. Try to remember what it was like to be a child or adolescent. For example, is he:

- Hungry?
- Lonely (wanting interaction)?
- Tired?
- Experiencing hormonal changes?
- Needing to be independent?
- Worried or scared because of family tension?

- Dealing with peer pressure?
- Stressed at school?
- Sick?
- Stressed by lack of routine, a new situation or other strain?
- Curious?

Once you think you have identified the need, it can be helpful to test your hypothesis. A direct statement such as, "I think you're hungry, is that right?" or "Would you like a sandwich right now?" is useful with many older children. Some children, especially toddlers, may just say "no" to anything. With them it may be better to offer the food: "Here's a sandwich."

When it is difficult to remember what it was like to be a child it can be helpful to watch children at play as they do their developmental "jobs" and/or you might want to read up on developmental stages. Sometimes when we have been raised in "too hot," "too cold," "too hard" or "too soft" environments, we never learn what normal is. It can feel like everyone else was given a manual at birth for a healthy childhood, but you never got your copy. Don't shame yourself for things you didn't learn. It is never too late to be a healthy parent.

Choices, Choices, Choices

It seemed to Hasan that any time three-year-old Yusef's wants were not fulfilled he would wail until he either got his way or would fall asleep from exhaustion. After mulling it over, Hasan realized that perhaps part of the problem was how little power young Yusef had over his life.

He wondered if Yusef would feel more powerful if he gave his son a choice. The next time Yusef whined and kicked, Hasan gave him a choice: "Yusef, you can go to your room and cry and scream, or you can sit here in the chair and quiet down." Remarkably it worked. Yusef chose the chair and relaxed.

After that, Yusef usually picked the chair. Occasionally, he went to his room, where he generally simmered down quickly. When Yusef wailed more then ten minutes, Hasan entered Yusef's room to offer other options: They could sit together in the rocking chair and read a book or he could just be held. Presenting choices worked nine times out of ten and helped Hasan build patience for when it wouldn't work.

When trying to elicit certain behavior from your child, use techniques that motivate:

- Offer a choice, so that your child may experience a degree of power in the situation: *"Would you like to clean up now, or finish your drawing and then clean up?" "We're leaving now. You may choose to walk with me or be carried."*
- Put things in a positive light: *"Please put your shoes in their place,"* rather than *"Don't throw your shoes in the living room."*

It is important to ask yourself, "What is a healthy way I can nurture my child's need?" You may need to take your child out of the current situation. For instance, if she is tired, it may be time to leave the restaurant even if you have not finished your meal. Acknowledge your own disappointment silently and remind yourself that with such small sacrifices you are planting the seeds of the future, which will benefit both of you.

If you can't think of a way to meet your child's need, simply acknowledge the need or emotion. If a child is old enough, it may be appropriate to ask him what he thinks would help. Of course, be prepared to say "no," if he wants a new Nintendo game that you are against buying!

It is very helpful for children to hear you name their emotions. Sometimes labeling the emotion—"It seems to me that you are frustrated" or "I know it can be frustrating when you can't put the pieces together"—helps your child to learn to articulate his or her own emotions. Physical and emotional growth happen at different rates. *Many experts consider that most children don't fully develop a psychological sense of self until approximately age eight.* Don't expect fast results. It takes time and being at the right developmental stage before your child is ready to express and name her own feelings.

When I'm one-on-one with Marlon's son Jamal I'm fine.

But as soon as Marlon walks into the room, everything falls apart. Jamal turns into a whining monster, Marlon tries to appease him, and I get mad!

But I'm not sure if I'm angry at **Jamal** for being a brat or **Marlon** for butting in. Or maybe I'm just mad at **myself**. I don't know who to blame!

It's bound to be one of the **usual suspects.**

Your Shoes Are Much Too Big

John excelled in math but never sports when he was young. He was determined that his son Caleb would never suffer the humiliation he'd experienced when it came time to choose teams. He coached Caleb in soccer, baseball and basketball from the sidelines. Soon he found himself getting angry at Caleb for missing a goal or dropping the ball. The more he pushed Caleb, the worse Caleb seemed to play. It became a vicious cycle: When Caleb missed a ball it brought back all of John's feelings of helplessness and shame from the past, and he reacted in anger. The angrier John got, the more balls Caleb missed.

It's important to examine your motives when expecting a child to perform. Expecting your child to win the glory that eluded you in order to rid yourself of shame, or even pushing your child beyond his desires or capabilities in order to win a scholarship, is unfair to everyone. You'll never be nine again and you cannot relive your childhood. You can be sad about that, but your child cannot make up for your lost childhood.

Tall Tales and Triggers

Another question you may wish to ask is "What don't I like about my child's behavior?" Is it something he's learned from you (that you need to change about yourself)? Is it a developmental stage? (Toddlers want to do things by themselves, but they need to be taught to protest or express their needs respectfully: "It's okay to feel frustrated but it's not okay to hit your sister.") Is there a way for you to model the appropriate behavior?

In order to best assess how your behaviors affect your child, you may wish to keep a journal for the next week. You can record:

- Your child's behavior that triggered you (he refused to eat)
- The story you tell yourself about the behavior (he's trying to annoy me)

- Your response (I yelled at him)
- A different story to tell yourself (he's not trying to annoy me; he's interested in playing with his new toys)
- A new way you'd like to respond (call my friend to tell her I'm running late; then, let him play with his toys longer and offer lunch again later) (Middelton-Moz, 2000)

With older children, it is often helpful to ask them what is causing their anger. You may find that things you do, such as rushing, raising your voice, fighting, ignoring them or breaking promises provoke them. Older children can be encouraged to keep their own anger journal:

- What makes me angry?
- How do I express my anger? (fight, slam doors, hit, retreat to my room, feel depressed)
- What other more constructive things can I do with my anger?

You may need to help your kids come up with new strategies for anger. Some useful strategies are:

- Talk to parents about a troubling situation, or if not parents, a grandma or grandpa, a favorite auntie or uncle, a trusted neighbor.
- Tell parents, "I need some time alone."
- Exercise.
- Take a walk.
- Express feelings through art.
- Eat healthy foods.

When your toddler is sobbing inconsolably because you've flushed the toilet instead of letting him do it himself, or your eight-year-old is picking a fight with her younger brother after you wrongly blamed her for something, remember:

- This isn't your first or last mistake. There is no such thing as a perfect parent.
- You can't completely protect your child from pain or disappointment.
- Over time your child will learn how to handle frustration and how to express anger appropriately.
- You and your child will get angry at each other—it's a natural part of life.
- Acknowledge your mistakes to your children. Apologize when you do something wrong.
- Think of the things you wanted to hear when your parents made mistakes that hurt you in your youth. Sometimes remembering your early desires and needs is helpful in knowing what to say to your children. Reach inside yourself for the wisdom and gifts that you have gleaned from difficult times in childhood.

You are your child's teacher, and a good teacher always learns something new from his or her pupils. Be open to the exchange and try to see parenting as an art, not a science; see each challenge as an opportunity for problem solving, not a test of your competence.

YOUR CHILD AND BULLYING

While you cannot protect your child from all the slings and arrows that life may throw, you can teach your child skills to make her less likely to become a victim of bullying. You can also give her strategies and tools to help her deal with the unhealthy anger of others.

It is important, too, that your child know he can talk to you about things that are bothering him. Try to pay attention to how your child is feeling. Look for any signs of being bullied such as lethargy or not wanting to go to school. Ask his teachers if he gets along with the children in class. In addition, if he knows you will treat him with respect, kindness and support, he will feel comfortable confiding in you. If you tend to dismiss his concerns, blame him for being bullied, or show disappointment in him for not standing up, he will find it hard to confide in you.

Bullies: Strategies for Survival suggests several strategies that help children be less vulnerable—becoming aware of their voice, posture, movements and overall presentation. The more confident and comfortable they seem, the less likely they are to be bullied. (Middelton-Moz, Zawadski, 2002)

The book *Bully-Proofing Your School* provides additional strategies including:

- Getting help from adults (teachers, parents, administrators)
- Asserting yourself (such as saying, "It's not okay to talk to me that way.")
- Using humor (making light of the situation, finding something funny to say that doesn't hurt others)
- Avoiding the bully (avoiding situations where you'll meet the bully; walking with friends when walking by the bully's house)
- Positive self-talk (helping your child to figure out his buttons and any negative messages he gives himself, helping him replace negative messages with positive ones)

- Owning your part of the experience (saying, "I'm sorry I bumped into you," acknowledges what you did) (Garrity, et al., 1994)

The most effective techniques for anti-bullying provide an environment where bullying behavior (by children or adults) is not tolerated. Instead of punishment, the bullies need to learn that their behavior is "bad" but they are not "bad people." Bullies need help rechanneling their energy.

Because anti-bullying really does take a whole community, teachers, students, staff, parents, etc., can be agents of change by helping their schools create effective anti-bullying programs. One of the most effective we've seen is the program detailed in *Bully-Proofing Your School*. In such an environment, all the staff, teachers and students at the school are taught the skills to create a caring community that does not tolerate bullying.

When students see bullying behavior, they are taught to speak out and obtain assistance from adults in the school. Children are given the skills to be able to share their feelings and experiences in an emotionally safe environment. Rather than creating power struggles with bullies, adult caregivers help them to channel their energies through using pro-social consequences instead of "punishment." When a child is bullied, he or she is able to take the situation to an adult who facilitates the creation of a safe environment for healing.

The child who has been bullied has an opportunity to speak to the caring school community about the effects of the bullying. In this way, the victim of bullying is not shamed, and the bully learns from the experience. The bully begins to learn empathy after seeing how his behavior has affected another. Instead of being shamed, the bully is helped by his or her caring community.

As you look to help your children and yourself with anger, remember that change takes time. Don't expect your child or yourself to change completely in one day. Model the right behavior and your child will imitate it over time. It may take a few days or a few weeks, but if you're consistent it will pay off. In terms of schools and community change, the process takes even longer. Take the long view and work towards change with others who share your vision.

Anger-obics^{SM}: Move Your Body, Shift Your Mind

Sounds Right!

Sometimes Lisa finds herself angry with her two-year-old son. He won't eat anything she offers, won't put on his shoes to go outside, runs away from her when she wants to change his diaper, or generally won't do what she thinks he should. She wants to scream in frustration, but knows that won't be good for him or her. So she makes a funny angry face and growls. He breaks out into laughter, and usually she does, too.

She feels better right away. She's letting him know in a very primitive way that she is feeling frustrated—the situation is not what she wants. At the same time, she's not engaging in an out-and-out battle of wills. She knows she's teaching him, too, that anger can be expressed without hurting someone. The great thing is that once they laugh, she's usually less attached to the outcome, and sometimes he is, too. She might find a creative solution now that she's not stuck in anger, or he may be more cooperative now that she changed the mood from one of coercion to one of fun.

Try this with a child or other family member. When you're angry, make an exaggerated angry face (you can always practice this face in the mirror now, in preparation for an occasion to use it). Then growl or bark or make a funny sound that expresses anger without scaring (not too loud and never rageful).

Lighten Up

Here's your chance to complain about relationships: with your kids, partner, parent(s), coworkers, friends, etc. Write each gripe, everything that makes you angry or frustrated or unhappy, on a separate index card or slip of paper.

Put all the cards or papers in a bowl. Place the bowl of gripes in a sunny spot for an entire week. Each morning notice the bowl in the daylight and imagine that the Golden Healing Light of the sun is helping to resolve each situation in some way.

At the end of the week, pick one complaint out of the bowl. Sit in a sunny spot. Close your eyes. Feel the golden healing light of the sun upon your face and give thanks for the sun and all the healing work the sun has been doing to resolve the issue.

With your inner eye, envision the piece of paper radiating with light. Hold the sheet of paper up to your heart imagining that the golden light is entering your heart now. As the light enters your heart, imagine that your feeling or perception of the situation has shifted. Allow an image to form in your mind's eye to symbolize this change.

When you are ready, open your eyes. Draw a picture of the symbol, or write a story about any change that has occurred in your perception of this issue.

Animal Crackers

Close your eyes. Return to the Golden Healing Light exercise from chapter 3 (if you prefer you can use Gratitude Attitude from chapter 2). Imagine the Golden Healing Light entering your being and creating a peaceful state. Imagine that in this peaceful state you can view your anger more clearly.

With your eyes still closed, imagine that your anger is an animal. What animal is it? Picture yourself in the wilderness in a place you might be likely to find your anger animal—on a mountain, in the woods, underwater, in a cave. Invite your anger animal to enter the scene. Note the details you can observe with all your senses: sight, smell, sound, etc. When you feel ready, open your eyes.

Describe your anger animal in detail or draw a picture. For example, "My anger is a lean and hungry bobcat with sharp teeth and long claws. It runs fast and chases people. I can hear it roar loudly."

What does your picture or description tell you about your anger?

_____

_____

_____

_____

Masquerade

Materials needed: Music (CD, tape), large paper plate, pencil, string or yarn, crayons, paints or markers, any other adornments you wish to use (stickers, buttons, glitter, ribbons, etc.). This exercise can be done alone, with a friend or with kids.

Part I:

Put on some music that you find expressive of anger or think of something that causes you to feel angry. Take a large paper plate. Place the plate in front of your face and mark, with a pencil, where your eyes fall. Now cut out holes for the eyes. Cut two holes on the sides for string.

The outside of the mask represents how you appear on the outside when you're feeling angry. When you flip the mask over, the inside represents how you feel inside.

You may want to close your eyes for a few minutes and take a few deep breaths as you picture in your mind's eye how your angry face appears to the world. Open your eyes. Using crayons, markers and any adornments, make a mask of how you might appear to others when you're angry. How does the mouth look? The eyebrows? The eyes? If you wish, you may choose to add hair with yarn or ribbon and adorn the mask with any ribbons, objects, materials, jewelry, etc. Tie a piece of string or yarn to each of the two holes on the sides.

Turn the mask over, close your eyes, take a few deep breaths into your belly and allow an image to form in your mind of how you're feeling on the inside when you're angry. Open your eyes and draw or paint the inside of the mask according to the image that formed.

When you're done, put on your mask, tying the string together in back of your head. Look in the mirror. What is your reaction?

Part II (Optional):

Playing the same music you played while making the mask or just with silence, begin your "anger dance" with your nondominant hand. Allow your hand to express anger that you hold in your body. When it feels right, have your other arm join the dance. Then add your shoulders. Now bring your hips and then your whole body into the dance.

You may wish to write about your experience below.

_____

_____

_____

_____

_____

_____

MAD PAD

THE THING THAT IMPRESSES
ME THE MOST ABOUT AMERICA IS
THE WAY PARENTS OBEY
THEIR CHILDREN.

—*King Edward VIII*

HAVING CHILDREN MAKES YOU NO
MORE A PARENT THAN HAVING A
PIANO MAKES YOU A PIANIST.

—*Michael Levine*
Lessons at the Halfway Point

CHAPTER 8

WE CAN WORK IT OUT:
Conscious Conflict

Arguments are not necessarily a bad thing. In an argument, people often display their passion, communicate and work for change. Conflict in a relationship is a sign of health. The trouble is, most fights aren't fair and people get hurt. This chapter will show you how to minimize the hurt and maximize your ability to communicate and build a loving, respectful partnership. If your fights are particularly passionate, the tools of this chapter can help create civility during conflict, while acknowledging the passion that makes your relationship fulfilling.

THE NATURE OF HEALTHY CONFLICT

Fair fighting is a skill developed in the 1960s by clinical psychologist George Bach and colleagues. Therapists continue to teach fair fighting, employing skillful communication and negotiation to air and resolve conflict in relationships. In his groundbreaking book, *The Intimate Enemy,* Bach showed that these techniques could create and support:

- A safe environment where issues are addressed and worked out
- A positive outcome for both parties
- A strong long-term relationship

As we thought about writing this chapter, we felt it was time to change the terminology. While "fair fighting" acknowledges that conflict exists in relationship, it also implies a fight: two opponents against each other. We think that it is time to look at conflict in a new light.

The term *conscious conflict* recognizes our ability to remain conscious, aware and responsible during the conflict. In addition, rather than seeing conflict as adversarial, "conscious conflict" appreciates that both people have the same ultimate goal: an enjoyable and fulfilling relationship with someone they care about. Below are some common myths about conflict and the truth behind them:

Myth	Truth
Conflict creates distance between people.	Conflict handled in a good way increases connection.
Conflict leads to lack of control.	Holding it in, or handling conflict poorly, can lead to lack of control.
Conflict leads to violence.	Conscious conflict leads to compromise, empowerment and peaceful resolution; feelings of powerlessness lead to violence.

When we participate in conscious conflict we air the issues that are affecting the relationship, causing anger, resentment or frustration. Once aired, we need to make sure we understand each other's point of view.

Then, it is critical to find a solution both people find amenable. The more creative we can be with finding a solution, the more likely that both parties will be happy.

Not surprisingly, after we came up with the term "conscious conflict," a search on the Web showed that this term was already in use by consultants, scientists, spiritual seekers, computer-software developers and even a financial consultant!

Gonna Take a Temperamental Journey

When Janice got angry, she usually felt out of control. Her tantrums were filled with trash talk, name-calling and accusations. A few times she even threw something; on different occasions she threw a book, a pumpkin and a vase. After a fight she always felt ashamed and apologized. It did not seem possible to her that she could change her behavior.

Carlos worried that Janice's attacks brought out the worst in him as he began to rage, too. When she threw a pot filled with chicken soup, it was the last straw. He issued an ultimatum: "Janice, I love you, but I can't live like this. It's either your rage or me."

Facing the loss of her marriage, Janice became willing to try to change. After two false starts they found an excellent couples' therapist whom they saw a dozen times. The therapist gave them many of the tools discussed later in this chapter, tools they used to break their old patterns.

Outside of the weekly sessions Carlos and Janice worked hard employing the tools to turn their fights into conscious conflict. There were days of backsliding, but each week brought dramatic improvement. Janice realized that raging was a behavior she had learned from her mother, not an inseparable part of her own personality. The tools of conscious conflict liberated her from her past.

Today, most of their issues are cleared up by honest discussion and good listening. Occasionally, name-calling or yelling occurs. They catch themselves quickly, apologize and work out the true issues behind the fight. Let's learn their secrets.

ESTABLISHING GROUND RULES

The Rules

Here are the rules for creating a safe environment:

- No violence
- No yelling at the other person
- No name-calling
- No fighting past the boiling point

Let's look at each of these rules in detail:

- **No violence.** This includes hitting, pushing, threatening, biting and throwing things. Even if someone is throwing things near another person but not directly at them, it can feel scary.
- **No yelling.** If you need to yell, go to a safe place (such as in the woods) to let out your feelings through yelling. In the disagreement itself, keep voices calm and at a moderate volume. As much as you are able, try to keep tension out of your voice. While yelling is normal to some people, others can feel very threatened and scared when voices are raised.
- **No name-calling.** Name-calling is a symptom of rage. When you call others names, you don't see them for who they truly are. You put people on the defensive, making it difficult for them to hear what's really

bothering you. Name-calling often escalates a fight. Sticking to facts and your own experience is easier to hear and leads more easily to resolution.

- **No fighting past the boiling point.** When one of you feels overwhelmed, triggered, unsafe or enraged, it is time to take a "time-out." If one person calls "time-out," both of you are required to comply. This means no talking to each other for two hours. You must physically separate from each other (separate rooms at least). In two hours you may come back to work things out, as long as you both have cooled off.

More About Time-Out

One reason a fight can soar into rage, and even violence, is that participants often become "hooked in" to their deepest rage from all their past experiences of helplessness. They are not living in the present moment and reacting to the issue at hand. Instead, they are overreacting, responding to injuries of the past. A time-out gives you time to get a little distance from the issue at hand, and from the past. Stepping away from the person gives you a chance to return to the present. From a biological viewpoint, a time-out gives your body a chance for the stress hormones to leave your bloodstream.

During a time-out, don't dwell on your rage. It can easily grow. Do something good for yourself. Take a walk in nature, write in a journal, draw a picture, do an *Anger-obics*ᔆᔐ exercise, practice yoga, bicycle, exercise, sing, pray or dance. Healthy exercise, creativity and meditative practices all help you reconnect with your strong and wise self. Then you can see the situation clearly and put your best resources into improving it. Physical exercise also releases the pent-up energy of anger.

What not to do when you take a time-out:

- Don't watch violent, provocative TV shows or videos, or shows, such as the news, that add to your feelings of helplessness.

- Don't drink alcohol, do drugs or overindulge in sweets.
- Don't obsess about the situation in your mind, getting more enraged.

Use the time-out as a TIME-OUT. You can use your *Mad Pad* to note some time-out strategies you'd like to try.

Success

When you first agree to the new ground rules, you may want to write them up as a contract: "I agree to _____." Include the rules listed in the beginning of this section.

If you are enraged and your partner calls "time-out," you may want to keep fighting. Remind yourself of your promise and take at least two hours away. Janice recalls, "I think I knew at some level that I was in a crazy space when I raged, but I couldn't stop myself. I depended on Carlos to call time-outs. Over time, we needed time-outs less and less. Time-outs saved our marriage."

Before a conversation or argument escalates, one of you may realize it's not a good time to talk. You're tired, engaged or enraged and need to break before things get out of control. It's fine to take a break, but address the issue soon. Negotiate a time to discuss the issue. For example, you can say, "This is an important issue. I will be better equipped to give it proper attention tomorrow. Can we revisit it first thing in the morning?"

TOOLS FOR MASTERING CONFLICT

Okay. You've broken the pattern of raging, but what patterns do you replace them with? You take the time-out, but what happens two hours later when you're back at the table?

Active Listening

There's a prayer attributed to St. Francis of Assisi: "Grant that I may not so much seek to be understood as to understand." What a powerful request! What would it be like to let go of what you want the other person to "get" and instead try to really hear what he or she wants you to hear?

One of our first mistakes in discussions or fights is that we are often so sure of what someone is trying to tell us that we've already decided what his point is before he completed his first sentence. Instead of listening, we're already thinking about our response to what we assume he is trying to say. Maybe we're even interrupting him before he finishes.

Try this experiment. Have your friend or partner tell you about something. Rather than respond, try to paraphrase what he is telling you. "I hear that you are . . ." or "Are you saying that . . . ?" Perhaps the person will say "yes," give more details or correct a misperception. In this case, try paraphrasing again and see if you understand yet. No? Keep trying. You may wish to switch roles and see how it feels to have someone truly listen to you. You can practice this tool regularly, so that when you do have a fight, it's easy to use and remember.

Taking Responsibility

One time-tested way of communicating is what we've nicknamed the "therapist's creed." Perhaps you've heard someone use it or maybe this tool is already in your toolbox. It goes like this, "When you _____ _____, I feel _____.
I need [or want] _____." What's so great about this way of communicating? There's no blame. You take responsibility for your interpretation

of events, your emotions and your actions. So instead of putting someone on the defensive, you're inviting him or her to be on your team.

Instead of hearing you say, "You made me _____," or "You hurt me by _____ _____," which causes a person to defend himself, you make it clear that you "own" your response to the situation.

One key for this to work is to make the "When you _____ " statement as clear a statement of fact as possible. For example:

"When you come home later than we planned . . ."
"When you drive over the speed limit . . ."

These statements work better than:

"When you make me angry . . ."
"When you don't think about me . . ."

The latter are your interpretations of the facts, but they are not the underlying facts. Stick to the facts with the "When you . . ." statement, then interpret with the "I . . ." statement:

"I feel hurt . . ."
"I feel frustrated . . ."
"I think you don't care . . ."

Make sure the "I feel . . ." is an emotion. Saying, "I feel like you don't love me," is confusing emotion with thoughts. The truth is that "I think you don't love me."

The last part of your statement is either a bottom line or a proposal. When you use "I need," you say, "This is a need I have, a bottom line. There may be repercussions if you can't meet that need." For example, "I need to hear that you care about my health." When you use "I want . . ." you are stating a preference and making a proposal. For example, "I want us to have a budget and discuss any purchases over $100 before spending."

When you . . . I feel . . . I need (or want) allows the person to:

- Respond to your experience:
  — "I didn't realize you felt that way."
  — "Yes, I was trying to hurt you because I felt hurt."
- Respond to your need or desire:
  — "I can meet that need."
  — "I can't meet that need."
  — "I don't want to do that, but I can do this instead . . ."

The person may try to negotiate a different solution from the one you proposed; take time to work out a compromise. Here's where it's crucial to remember active listening and the rules for conscious conflict.

The Third-Party Animal

Sometimes you need to express yourself to a neutral third person who can just "hear you out." Perhaps your boss treated you unfairly or you're angry about a societal injustice and you need to:

- Let go of some of the frustration or anger
- Work things through to figure out how you want to respond
- Get feedback on your part/responsibility
- Get feedback on whether or not you are in a safe situation
- Get emotional support

Talking it through with a third party is different from gossiping or triangulating. In the latter, you are trying to hurt the person with whom you are angry by indirectly involving someone else. With healthy venting you are giving voice to anger or frustration in order to get feedback, reach clarity and, perhaps, let it go. Talking it through with a third party doesn't include yelling, name-calling or violent images. Try to stick to the facts and why you are angry.

Often, after talking it through, it can be appropriate to come up with a strategy for approaching the person who offended you and taking action with that person. In some cases, such as sexual harassment, it may make more sense to address the issue through a third party, such as a human-resources manager or even an attorney. In these cases, trusted friends and mentors can help you make a decision as to which course is best.

It was common in the '70s and '80s to encourage people to vent by physical actions, such as hitting a punching bag with a baseball bat or punching a pillow while yelling. Today, research shows that this type of venting rehearses anger.

REACHING CLOSURE

You've had your time-out. You've made your "when you . . . I feel . . . I need . . ." statement. Your partner has offered a solution. If you like your partner's suggestion you're done, right? Not exactly. There's still time to screw up! Make sure you agree on the solution. You may want to even put it in writing. It's also helpful to agree to revisit the issue in a week or so to see if you are both satisfied with the outcome. If not, try to figure out why it isn't working:

- Are you both complying?
- Did you have different understandings of the agreement?
- Is one of you unhappy with the agreement? If so, you need to figure out why you are unhappy with it and/or renegotiate the agreement.

It's one thing to work towards closure with someone who's agreed to conscious conflict, but how do you achieve closure in other situations? What if your partner refuses to use the rules of conscious conflict? What if your boss uses her power improperly? What if your teenager is abusive?

In situations where someone is abusing his or her power and you don't expect that person to fight fair, you need to take care of yourself to reach closure.

Here's a brief guide for self-care:

Get Safe. What do you need to create safety? Examples are:

- Ask a third party for support.
- Get out of your living situation.
- Document the situation. Then call upon the courts (get a lawyer).
- Call the police when in danger or threatened.
- Brainstorm alternatives with a trusted friend.

Get Help. Bullies get away with bullying when the culture (corporate, family or societal) allows them to. Try to get the help you need for a fair outcome and to get the bully to stop his/her behavior. For example, if a boss is bullying employees:

- Does the bully have a superior who will be open to hearing your grievances?
- Is there a human-resources department to handle the grievance?
- Are there several peers or employees willing to confront the bully together?
- Is this a situation where you need legal counsel?

The Road to Recovery

When you take responsibility for your perceptions and reactions, you are on the road to health and greater happiness. You no longer see yourself as a victim. You know you have the power to change your life. When you work together with someone to change unhealthy patterns together, as in the case of conscious conflict, your relationship becomes more intimate, more satisfying and, often, more fun.

[AUTHORS' NOTE: In the heat of an argument, you may need some fast and accessible help. *Voilà!* We have summarized the rules of conscious conflict in appendix A. You may wish to photocopy the appendix and place it somewhere for easy reference. See appendix B for an example of two people using conscious conflict.]

Anger-obics^SM: Move Your Body, Shift Your Mind

Choosy Mothers Choose

Is there a situation where you have a million and one gripes? Do you hit the person over the head with everything you can possibly say about the situation? Rather than going great guns, you can think about the situation ahead of time.

Write down all the things you think you want to say. Now decide which one, two or three points are most important. Can you let go of the others, at least for the time being, in order to stay focused and not overwhelm the person?

_____

_____

_____

_____

_____

_____

_____

_____

Sherlock Holmes

This exercise can help you develop empathy for the other person during an argument. It can help you find common ground, improve communication and find better solutions that make both parties happy. Perhaps you can discuss the exercise with a sibling, partner, or other person you trust, and agree ahead of time to try this when you can't agree on something or find yourselves in an argument (probably one that's not hugely contentious).

Pretend you are a detective trying to understand the other person's motivations and side of things. Have the person talk to you about the issue as if you were a third party. Change the name of the person from yours to a fake name, so you don't feel so embroiled. It is important to stick to the facts: no name-calling or blaming.

As the person talks you are gathering information as you listen to the story. Rather than react to what the person is saying, even if you think he or she is misunderstanding your motives or actions, try to hear what he or she is saying. Does the person seem to be experiencing any specific emotions you can identify, such as fear, resentment, frustration, etc.? Can you see why he or she feels the way he or she does?

Does there seem to be any meeting ground? Anything you can agree on? For example, "I know we don't agree about whether or not to get Mom involved. I do see that it could be frustrating for you when I involve Mom without letting you know first. Next time I will give you a heads up."

What's So Funny About Peace, Love and Understanding?

This exercise uses a powerful technique called "active listening." If you have ever observed two people in an argument, you may have noticed them talking past each other, not hearing or knowing what the other one is saying. Active listening is the remedy for this situation. Active listening can seem a bit awkward at first, but you will soon appreciate its effectiveness. You probably will want to discuss the technique with the other person before putting it into practice.

1. Paraphrase what you think the person is saying.
2. Allow the person the opportunity to confirm or clarify what he or she is saying.
3. If the person has added a clarification, paraphrase that, too.
4. Once the person confirms that you have understood, you can then express your reaction.
5. Now it's the other person's turn to paraphrase and make sure he or she understands you.

Here's an example of how it works:

Friend: I was so angry yesterday when you slammed the door and yelled at me for being late. I was stuck in traffic and couldn't have arrived sooner.

You: You're saying I had no right to be angry?

Friend: No, I'm saying that I was stuck in traffic and couldn't have arrived sooner. You should have asked me about my situation.

You: Are you saying that you're angry that I slammed the door and yelled at you without first asking why you were late?

Friend: Yes. I was stuck in traffic. It was impossible to get there on time.

You: Are you saying that there was no way for you to get to me on time?

Friend: Yes.

You: I understand that you feel you couldn't control your lateness. However, it's the third time this week you've been late. I don't think it's all the fault of traffic. I think you don't give yourself enough time to travel, and I'm tired of your excuses.

Friend: You don't like my excuses.

You: That's right. Also, I think you don't give yourself enough time to get here; maybe you can leave some extra time in case there's traffic.

Friend: I hear you saying . . . etc.

One great thing about this exercise is that it forces both parties to listen to each other and really clarify what each of them is saying. It makes it much clearer to both parties what the argument is about. And it also tends to slow down the whole argument, so that things don't escalate and get nastier. People also tend to feel much better once they feel they are being understood.

Find a friend who is willing to discuss a misunderstanding or point of contention in this way. Have the friend speak first and try to see if you understand what he or she is saying. When your friend indicates that you have understood completely, switch roles.

Part-toons

Imagine that you and your partner are fighting over a money issue. (If you don't have a partner, think of a former partner, a friend or a relative.) Imagine you and your partner as superheroes, characters from a novel, famous actors or cartoon characters. Who are you? Your partner? What might these characters do in this situation?

If you wish, draw a stick figure or rough sketch of the characters. Above their heads write what they are saying. Add the circle around the words and a line to the person's mouth and you've created a cartoon. Feel free to add more "frames," that is, draw out the conversation that the two characters have.

Did the cartoon characters give you any ideas about another way you might respond to the situation? Was it helpful? Not helpful? There's no right or wrong answer.

MAD PAD

_____

_____

_____

_____

_____

_____   AN EYE FOR AN EYE
                                                        ENDS UP MAKING
_____   THE WHOLE WORLD BLIND.
                                                        — *Mahatma Gandhi*
_____

_____

_____

_____

> IF YOU WANT TO MAKE PEACE,
> YOU DON'T TALK TO YOUR FRIENDS.
> YOU TALK TO YOUR ENEMIES.
>
> — *Moshe Dayan*

CHAPTER 9

I CAN SEE CLEARLY NOW:
Healthy Anger

When anger drives us forward, rather than leaving us stuck in powerlessness, we become empowered in our personal lives. We become catalysts for change, making a difference in the lives of others. Our anger can ignite our desire to learn more, teach others, illuminate issues and join with others to fight injustice.

In this chapter, you will see how anger can be used to transform an unacceptable situation into a better one. We explore creativity and humor as two of the many ways of expressing anger in a healthy manner. We address anger as a natural and crucial step in the process of grieving. You will have the opportunity to develop your own plan for dealing with and expressing anger in healthy ways. We will guide you step-by-step as you experiment with different skills as you discover what works best for you. At the end of the chapter, we examine how our anger can be part of creating communities that are safe and inclusive.

ANGER AS MOTIVATION FOR MAKING A DIFFERENCE

In 1979, Laura Lamb and her mother Cindi were hit head-on by a repeat drunk-driving offender in Maryland. Five-and-a-half-month-old Laura became one of the world's youngest quadriplegics. Months later, in California, thirteen-year-old Cari Lightner was killed at the hands of a drunk driver who had a history of drunken-driving convictions yet, incredibly, still carried a valid California driver's license. Enraged, Cindi's mother on one side of the United States and Cari's mother, Candace, on the other, began mobilizing others to wage a war against drunk driving.

Candace Lightner gathered with friends at a steakhouse in Sacramento and discussed forming a group named MADD—Mothers Against Drunk Drivers. By the end of 1981, Cindi and Candace had joined forces and MADD became a name that swept the nation with more than seventy chapters operating by the fall of 1982. By MADD's tenth anniversary, the organization had grown to include 407 chapters internationally with 53 community-action teams. Shortly thereafter, a Gallup survey proclaimed drunk driving as the No. 1 problem on the nation's highways. Before the dawn of 2001, MADD had more than 600 chapters and community action teams in all fifty states with affiliates internationally. (Lord, 2000)

The overwhelming grief of two mothers sparked the birth of MADD which was instrumental in forever changing societal attitudes and legislation regarding drunk driving. This organization and countless others demonstrate that anger doesn't have to be a destructive emotion but rather one that has fueled positive and constructive reforms in society. Anger transformed into empowerment has brought about positive changes in the form of child labor laws, spousal and child abuse legislation, minority rights legislation, aid and overwhelming support for the ravished victims of war, terrorism and disease. Miraculously, many courageous family members of both the victims and perpetrators of drive-by shootings have transformed what could have become a lifetime of hate to join forces in order develop programs to stop a common enemy: gang violence.

THE HEALING POWER OF HUMOR

Study after study points to humor as one of the most effective coping methods we have. When we refer to humor, we are not talking about angry jabs disguised as a joke, the hurtful statement followed by "just kidding," or laughing and telling others it's all right when it isn't. We're talking about the experience of deep in the gut laughter and the ability, at times, to stand back and look at ourselves and find humor in our behavior. As exemplified in the cartoons in this book, our thoughts and actions are pretty funny sometimes. "Freud's definition of wit—a sudden illumination of truth—is, in fact, true to its etymology (the word is derived from Old English roots for thinking or knowing)." (Vaillant, 1977) Sometimes in humor, we see the truth of ourselves.

Parents, teachers and role models who nurture a sense of humor in children may be equipping them with one of the most important coping mechanisms for making it through stressful times throughout life. Our capacity for humor allows balance and can be a regulator for emotions; allows us to handle difficult times and situations without becoming emotionally exhausted; can provide a needed release from tension and anger; and enables us to broaden the horizon enough to see things from a different perspective.

Taking Hospitality a Step Too Far

Jane had been traveling on a particularly stressful speaking tour. Planes had been delayed; reservations were messed up. In one city, the desk clerk informed her that he didn't have a room for her. "But I have a reservation," she replied. "Sorry, there's a speaker everyone's here to see, and we have no rooms." "I'm that speaker," she said hopefully. With that, he set her up in a cot by the podium for the night.

Things went from bad to worse at the next city. An exhausted Jane arrived at the hotel desk for a large conference. She waited thirty minutes for her check-in. The bellman was nowhere to be found, so she lugged her two heavy suitcases to the elevator. When she opened the door to her room, there was a stark naked man on the bed. She slammed the door and lugged the suitcases back downstairs.

Back at the desk, Jane waited with the heavy suitcases—another half hour wait and, finally, a chance to tell her story. With forced calm in her voice she stated, "There's a naked man in my bed—no luggage, no clothes, just him." "That's impossible," answered the desk clerk, "my computer shows the room is free."

"I know a naked man when I see one." By now, Jane was not quite as calm as she'd been. The desk clerk called security and a large, skeptical man accompanied Jane back to the room. Sure enough, there was the naked man. "George, we've been looking for you everywhere." George was the missing bell captain!

News traveled fast: As other conference speakers heard about Jane's plight, they gathered in her room, irate about the naked bell captain. Jane's head pounded, and she felt angry at everyone—the hotel, the bell clerk and the well-intentioned, but shouting, speakers in her room.

At that moment, the conference manager calmly put her hand on Jane's shoulder. "Jane, I think we may have overlooked the obvious here. Maybe this is how the hotel welcomes you instead of a chocolate on the pillow."

Jane laughed so hard she really did cry. After the tears and laughter, her headache was gone and, miraculously, so was her anger. She ushered her friends out of the room and slept like a baby that night.

Laughter is one of the greatest gifts we can give ourselves. There is increasing evidence that humor improves our health as well as speculation that tears of laughter, like those of sorrow, may rid the body of harmful toxins. (Frey, 1985) Next time you're taking yourself and everyone else way too seriously, go to the video store and rent some comedies or call up your funniest friend. You'll lift your spirit and add to your emotional and physical well-being.

ANGER AND CREATIVITY

Degas once said, "A painter paints a picture with the same feeling as that with which a criminal commits a crime." Millions are spent on the criminal, the person who often continues to repeat the violence once directed at him or acts out the rage felt toward an unkind word. Not nearly enough time and energy is spent rewarding the resiliency, courage and power of the person who picks up a paintbrush or pen instead of a weapon.

In an interview with Steven A. Diamond, Ph.D., a clinical and forensic psychologist and author, Diamond states that an artist "can be understood as someone who strives to express him or herself creatively rather than destructively. I see it as a conscious choice one makes in life to aspire either toward the light or the dark, positive or negative, the creative or the constructive. The artist—be it the actor, musician, painter, play-wright, poet, novelist or simply a person who lives life very creatively—is able to give voice to his or her demons constructively rather than acting them out." He refers to creativity as "one of humankind's healthi-est inclinations, one of our greatest attributes." (Eby, 2003)

Through creativity we can use the safety of our imaginations to rearrange the details of our lives. When we use our creative energy we can give ourselves the freedom to plunge into and explore our deepest feelings through clay, dance, sound, words, crayons, scraps of material, colored paper, clippings from magazines or paints on a canvas. We can look at our problems and emotions from many different perspectives, rearrange, combine, synthesize and change our point of reference. It is a misconception that one has to be "artistically tal-ented," or be expert at drawing, painting or writing poetry to be creative. You can explore transforming your anger into creative energy and discover unexplored parts of yourself in many of the *Anger-obics*ˢᴹ exercises, or create your own exercises to creatively give your anger a sound, movement, a face, a shape or a texture.

ANGER AND GRIEF

Anger is a necessary step in the process of grieving. Grief is the rainbow of intense feelings associated with a loss or misfortune. The expression of grief is mourning. Grief and mourning are a normal and natural response to loss. Everyone experiences losses throughout their lives: death of a loved one; a divorce; death of a pet; loss of health, culture, home or language; loss of friendship, safety, innocence; loss of children through divorce, foster care, miscarriage, abortion, adoption; loss of parents through divorce, adoption or death; loss of trust, faith or spontaneity; loss of physical emotional, mental or financial well-being, etc.

James Pennebaker, Ph.D. conducted countless studies over a fifteen-year period with hundreds of people suffering a wide range of losses. He found that people who did not engage in a healthy grief process obsessed and ruminated continually, showed increased health risks, were under continual stress, displayed more aggressiveness and showed increases in addictions. (Pennebaker, 1997)

Many writers on the subject of grief have identified stages of the grieving process. Perhaps one of the best known is Elisabeth Kübler-Ross, M.D., who originally wrote about the five stages of grief: denial and isolation; anger; bargaining; depression; acceptance. (Kübler-Ross, 1969)

Sometimes, when bad things happen, people like to pretend nothing happened. Those who are grieving need to hear others speak the truth of what occurred: "I'm sorry to hear you have cancer." Support, of course, is critical to the grieving process. It is also helpful to hear others acknowledge the feelings: "You must feel very sad" or "I can understand you feel angry." Seeing a tear in someone else's eye can be the very thing that helps a person grieve. It takes time for individuals to move through the many facets of grief on the road to healthy resolution:

- Denial and numbing
- Physical responses
- Emotional release
- Panic and confusion
- Guilt
- Hostility and anger
- Regression
- Social sharing
- Acceptance
- Regaining present and future focus

Of the many stages of healthy grieving, anger is one of the least understood and least tolerated in ourselves and others. Many of us learned throughout our lives that "good people" are not angry, or that anger is a destructive emotion that must be avoided at all cost. Many believe the myth that it is unimaginable and abnormal to be angry with a loved one who has died. It is normal to be angry at the unfairness of it all: the person who has left us, institutions, God, mistakes, those we hold responsible, or sometimes all of humanity for a time.

Anger is a healthy emotion that arises when we feel threatened emotionally, physically or mentally. Healthy anger allows us to prepare ourselves emotionally and physically in times of perceived danger. Healthy anger is our natural protection against hurt. Healthy anger, therefore, is a normal reaction when there is loss. Underneath the anger and hostility are usually the natural feelings of vulnerability, helplessness and fear that accompany loss.

Anger is not the problem. It is what we do with our anger that may be a problem. Because anger seems "abnormal" during grief, many have a tendency to repress their anger, which can lead to depression, or to act it out against others, most commonly those we love. If we don't "talk it out," we have a tendency to "act it out." The expression of healthy anger is a critical part of healthy grieving. When we can accept our anger as a normal and necessary reaction to loss, we can express it in healthy and responsible ways.

If you need to grieve, talk to others about your feelings, including anger. You may also use some of the creative means discussed earlier (painting, writing, drawing, clay, etc.) to explore your anger and grief.

CREATING NEW PATTERNS: A STEP-BY-STEP PROCESS

Many books can give you a three-step-system (or four or five steps) to fix a problem. With anger, different people have different styles that work for them. In this exercise, you get to try out different responses and invent your own three-step plan for dealing with anger. Here's the outline:

1. **Break the Pattern:** Notice that you're angry and about to do your usual anger response. Instead choose to deviate from your usual behavior and do something else instead.
2. **Identify and Evaluate:** Figure out what's really going on for you. Ask yourself, "Am I reacting only to the current situation, or are there things about this situation that remind me of the past? If the latter is true, what about the past is triggering me? How can I separate the past from the present in this moment?" Seek support to share and process your feelings.
3. **Take Action.** Respond in a healthy way to the person with whom you are angry.

Step 1: Break the Pattern

There are many tools one can use to break the pattern: One way to break a pattern is to take a few deep breaths, or to count to ten. These strategies can work especially well if you're in a situation where you can't easily take a break: For example, if your toddler is throwing a tantrum about leaving the playground, you need to remain with her. You may also wish to repeat a few words you've chosen to remind yourself that your child is not trying to drive you into the loony bin. "Jessica is finding it hard to leave the playground. She is not out to get me!"

If this doesn't work, try changing your focus: Look away from the person or sing some calming song lyrics in your head, such as "If you're angry and you know it, stomp your feet" (to the tune of "If You're Happy and You Know It").

Some people need physical space to change the pattern. By moving away from the person or situation, you can gain perspective. You can take a step back, stand up (if you're sitting) or walk away (usually it helps to let the person know that this is what you're doing). You may want to plan a time to revisit the issue with the person.

Here are some possible things to say when walking away:

- "I want to discuss this, but I need time to cool down. Let's meet back here in an hour."
- "This is getting intense. Let's take a two-hour time-out."
- "I've got to go. I'll be happy to discuss this tomorrow morning."
- "I need time alone right now to sort things out. Can we talk later?"

If you take time alone, it may be helpful to focus on something else: Take a few deep breaths, meditate, get physical exercise such as a bike ride or walk. Afterwards you can return to the issue and step 2.

Taking a time-out is a very important tool. It gives your body time to get out of the stress response and the physiological changes that are causing agitation. If you use the time to do something physical, the body's stress energy is released through exercise. If you do something calming, you can return to a relaxed state, as well. In a relaxed state, it is much easier to get clarity about the situation, and to bring the wisdom of your mind, body, emotions and spirit to bear on the issue, rather than just going with a strong emotional response.

It is important to note that your body will need at least twenty minutes for the stress hormones to clear. For some people, it may even be longer. If you use the time to stew and brew over your anger, the time-out won't do you any good. Instead it will create a cycle of negative thoughts and feelings.

There are times when it may work better for you to talk to a third party. Healthy venting does not include yelling, name-calling or violent images. If you find yourself venting on a daily basis, your venting is probably not a constructive pattern. Are you feeling powerless, like a victim, when you vent? If so, this is an issue you may wish to address with a counselor, therapist or other healing practitioner. Note which tools for breaking the pattern appeal to you most and write them on your *Mad Pad*.

Step 2: Identify and Evaluate

Ask: "Is my reaction out of proportion to what happened?" If you're not sure you know the answer to this question, ask a neutral third party. Other questions include: "Am I living in this time zone or is there something about the past that comes into play and colors my experience? Am I mad at someone in my past in a way that is creeping into the present situation?"

If some past issue is cropping up, see if you can find a way to separate past from present. It is helpful to sort this out with a trusted friend or support person. Once you realize you are triggered by the past, you may find that your anger at the current situation or person has lessened:

1. Identify the facts of the current situation; not opinion, just what happened. (For example, "Maura invited Amanda and Akira to go to the movies, but didn't call me.")
2. Identify what you are feeling: angry, hurt, frustrated, sad, afraid, etc.
3. Ask yourself, "Is this a familiar feeling? When else have I felt this way?"
4. Identify any past triggers, situations or people that seem to be coming up in this situation.
5. You may want to write about the past and present issues, or talk to someone, a counselor or friend. If you are more visual than verbal, visualize each issue as being contained in a different color box, or visualize yourself placing the past issue on a shelf to be dealt with later. Now bring your focus to the present.

There are different methods people use to identify and evaluate. Here are some you can try:

- Write in a journal.
- Go to a quiet place and think.
- Talk to a trusted friend or mentor.

- Talk with a counselor or therapist.
- Pray or meditate.
- Try an *Anger-obics*ᔆᴹ exercise that seems well suited for identifying and evaluating the issues.

You can write any ideas for this step on your *Mad Pad*.

Step 3: Take Action

Here are several different ways you can take action depending on the situation and your ability to trust the person; some can be combined:

- Talk to the person about your concerns. Try to negotiate a solution.
- Write the person about your concerns.
- Decide how you will change your perspective to address the issue.
- Remove yourself from the offending situation (please consider whether you are running away from the situation [not effective] or leaving an unhealthy and unworkable situation [effective]):
  — Start looking for another job, roommate, etc.
  — Leave your home situation, if it is untenable.
  — Spend time with people who treat you better.
- Get support for meeting your needs.
- Do something to change the situation:
  — Write a note apologizing for your part in the conflict.
  — Spend less time with the person or temporarily stop seeing him or her.

If the situation is political or societal, here are some other ways to change things:
- Send money to a charity that helps people in a similar situation.
- Write to your congressperson to support a bill that will help bring about change in a specific area.
- Boycott a company whose policies you don't approve of.
- Start an organization that will work to change whatever is vexing you.

Again, it may be helpful to use your *Mad Pad* for ideas about this step.

CREATING PEACEFUL COMMUNITIES

We continue to work on our personal anger throughout our lives. Nobel Peace Prize nominee and Buddhist monk/teacher Thich Nhat Hanh reminds us that we will never be rid of anger. Anger will continue to visit each of us. Our real challenge is to greet our anger with awareness and love.

As you practice new skills and gain insights, you will become more proficient, improving your experiences of:

- Understanding anger's message
- Communicating the need behind the anger
- Meeting your needs

As you continue on your path of personal growth, we encourage you to have patience with yourself. Sometimes you will do the "Bunny Hop" (two steps backward and three steps forward).

As you become more skillful, you will find yourself with opportunities to share your insights and skills with others. We encourage you to ask the following questions:

- Is there a role for anger in improving our society?
- How can I come to terms with the anger I find in groups and organizations that are supposed to be helping create a better and more peaceful world?
- How can I help make my community a place of healthy, not unhealthy, anger?

Anger in Community Groups

"Another awful conservation board meeting?" Evelyn asked, as Keiko slammed the door on her way in. "I was so excited when I joined," Keiko replied wearily, "but that Mavis Travis drives me nuts. She took credit for my idea to form a small business association to fight the new development and preserve Willett's Marsh. Now they've elected her chair. She's alienated so many people with her pushiness. I think we're going to lose the battle."

Many times we join a group or organization in order to do good and better our community. Whether it be to volunteer in a hospital, conserve land, promote economic development, help disadvantaged youth, share our spiritual ideals or protect animals, our common goal couldn't be a better one . . . or so it seems. However, we too often find ourselves at odds with our fellow "do-gooders."

Volunteering time and effort usually represents a sacrifice in a busy life. In work situations, people are motivated to get along by considerations of income and career. Most people understand that if they throw a

hissy fit at work and quit, they will face consequences. In community groups, people don't have those same external incentives to work things out.

One especially hurtful and divisive expression of anger that occurs within communities is gossip. Gossip might seem like a relatively harmless practice, but, unchecked, gossip can wreak havoc on people and organizations. Gossip can undermine trust and integrity, encourage divisiveness, and rip apart the very allegiances that bind most groups together. At its worst, gossip is a passive-aggressive form of violence that hurts, causes further alienation and isolation, and strengthens oppression. (Middelton-Moz 1999) When people are oppressed, they sometimes use gossip as a "safe" way to vent their frustrations and sense of powerlessness. The result, however, is that they rob themselves of their most valuable resource: each other.

If someone in your group or community is a gossip, don't participate. Tell the gossiper that she must talk to the person about whom she's gossiping directly, and that you won't listen. If you notice others gossiping, speak up and express your discomfort. Encourage open and honest communication about differences, and refuse to tolerate back-stabbing and rumor-spreading.

We're all human. Belonging to a well-intentioned cause doesn't mean we've worked out all our issues. The more passionate someone is about an issue, the more entrenched that person might be in his or her own view. People who promote altruistic agendas aren't automatic candidates for sainthood—almost all groups, from local nonprofits to multinationals, grapple with issues of bullying, power struggles, abuse of authority and internal conflict.

Here's what you can do:

- Keep the long view: Remember you're supporting the same cause. Try to have compassion for the person. She may not have dealt with her own personal issues and is doing her best.

- If you think someone is acting inappropriately, try to talk with her first, away from the group, to see if you can hear each other in a place where no one is made to feel embarrassed. Use some of the skills you've learned to communicate effectively without blame.
- If the person can't hear you, it may be necessary to take action. Suggest positive ways for the group to handle conflict:
  — Active Listening: Use a talking stick at a meeting—only the person with the stick (or other object) can speak while others listen. After a designated time, the stick gets passed to the next speaker.
  — Make sure everyone has a copy of *Robert's Rules of Order,* and remind people to follow those rules for respectful and effective meetings.
  — Suggest an agenda with times printed on it. If discussion goes beyond the time frame, the group can vote to continue or move on.

If the person is using manipulation and other bullying tactics, remember that bullies rely on those around them to be too cowed, apathetic or self-serving to intervene. The group must work together to keep bullies from harming others or undermining a worthy cause. Stand up to bullies: Look them in the eye and use confident body language. Keep your comments to the point, and don't use absolutes. Remember that when you act helpless or fight, the bully achieves power.

When dealing with difficult people inside your organization, remember that your anger can be effective and forceful if you focus on ideas and organizational goals instead of personalities. Act with respect and remember you both are striving for similar outcomes—build consensus on that common foundation.

. . . Divided We Fall

Often groups in a community are at odds with each other over fundamental differences. Opinion can be bitterly divided over issues such as abortion rights, gun control and zoning. Our beliefs arise from core convictions about who we are and the kind of society we desire. Not only is it difficult to view heartfelt ideologies from a dispassionate viewpoint, it can feel like a betrayal of principle. To move from anger at a doctrine to anger at the doctrine's advocate can seem like barely moving at all.

Is it appropriate to feel anger at someone who promotes an agenda you feel is unethical or immoral? It's almost impossible not to. Anger is a normal reaction—purposeful anger often arises in response to injustice or inequity. Most situations are not all black or all white.

R-E-S-P-E-C-T

After Senator Paul Wellstone was tragically killed, his staunch opponent Senator John McCain eulogized him as an idealist who fought hard for his beliefs but always operated in a context of respect. Respect is the key. Attempt to establish a shared language with your opponent and areas where compromise might be possible. Allow a diversity of voices. Compassionately confront those who preach hate or violence. Fight ideas, not people, and accept the basic tenet that community life is a partnership. Your anger can become a powerful force for creating a community where inclusion and diversity are valued.

When we witness an injustice or the violation of a principle, healthy anger can give us the courage to act, not react. Productive anger can be a guide to appropriate, powerful and healing action.

What you can do to promote healthy and productive interactions:

- Practice tolerance: You don't have to agree with diverse views, but you can accept that other people have the right to their opinions.

- Encourage an energetic but respectful debate of issues.
- Refuse to tolerate bullying or any other hurtful behavior. Seek support when confronting bullies.
- Support accountability and personal responsibility on all levels.
- Promote inclusion instead of discrimination.
- Practice courtesy, fairness and justice.
- Recognize that through processing healthy anger you can articulate the need for worthwhile change.

All the great political and social movements of our time are rooted in healthy anger: the struggle against apartheid, the fight for civil and women's rights, living-wage actions, healthy food initiatives, nonviolent resistance, many environmental and animal-protection movements. The founders of these movements experienced healthy anger against conditions they considered to be unjust and unacceptable. They expressed their anger through voice and action. They proved to be an irresistible force for change. You, too, can be a voice for positive change. Perhaps you already are!

Anger-obics^{SM}: Move Your Body, Shift Your Mind

Role Models

Think of someone you admire who has taken an angry situation and used his or her anger in a nonviolent way to create social or political change. For example, Dr. Martin Luther King Jr., who championed civil rights; Mahatma Gandhi, who inspired King and brought together a country; or Julia "Butterfly" Hill who sat in a tree for a year to keep a logging company from cutting down old growth forest and who succeeded in getting a great deal of attention for the issue of clear-cut logging. (Note: You don't have to agree with Hill's politics to appreciate how she used her anger to meet her goals in a nonviolent way.)

Draw a picture or stick figure of this person you admire and a picture or stick figure of yourself. Imagine yourself asking this person for advice on a societal issue that upsets you, such as education, taxes, the environment, corporate corruption, politics, whatever. Write a question above the picture of you and a circle around the words with a line going to your mouth, creating a cartoon caption.

Draw the two of you again. This time, imagine what the person might say back to you as advice and write that out as a cartoon caption. If it is helpful, you can use Gratitude Attitude or the Golden Healing Light meditation to get into a meditative space and then ask the question of your "hero."

If you want, you can draw a third "frame" for your cartoon, and show yourself replying to the person. Has this exercise given you any ideas for reframing the issue or taking action?

Walk to the Beat

When you need to take a break at work because of anger, when you're taking a time-out, or when you're just angry and needing to move, try this. Choose a piece of music that expresses how your anger feels. Play it on a Walkman® as you walk to its beat.

You can describe your experiences here:

_____

_____

_____

_____

_____

_____

_____

_____

Passion in Action

When you listen to the news on TV or the radio, do you ever feel angry or powerless? Which news themes trigger you? Corporate dishonesty? Abused children? Environmental pollution? Left-wing/right-wing politicians? Think of one of these issues that trigger your anger or your powerless feelings and write about what upsets you the most about this issue.

Write down one or two things you can do about the issue (for example, write your congressman, boycott a company, write a company president, contact your local newspaper, encourage friends to boycott, donate to a charity that trains parents to use alternatives to violence, etc.).

Sit comfortably in a chair or on the floor with your spine straight. Close your eyes. Do the Gratitude Attitude exercise from chapter 2 or the Golden Healing Light exercise from chapter 3.

At the end of the meditation, as you picture yourself calm and grateful or filled with the golden healing light, rise to a standing position. Stand straight with your feet firmly planted on the floor, hip-width apart. Imagine a ball of energy in the area of your solar plexus (below your ribs and above your belly button). Imagine that this ball of energy gives you the power to act and make positive changes in the world. As you breathe in, focus on the powerful positive energy of this ball. As you breathe out, feel its positive power within yourself.

Now picture yourself taking action on the issue in one of the ways that you wrote about. In your mind's eye, picture that the situation is somehow changed by your action, that your action has made a positive difference. You may want to picture one particular person being helped by your actions. Notice how your body feels. When you feel you are done, bring your attention back to your feet on the floor, back to the room you are in, and open your eyes if they were closed.

Write any notes here and then take action!

_____

_____

_____

_____

_____

_____

_____

_____

_____

Blast from the Past

Part I:

What are your experiences of anger from childhood? What are your associations and preconceptions of anger (check the examples that apply and add your own):

❍ Only jerks like my _____ get angry and express their anger.

❍ Expressing your anger makes people hate you.

○ You won't have friends if you express your anger.

○ Anger is dangerous.

○ Feeling angry makes me a bad person.

○ If I allow myself to feel angry I will hurt someone.

○ Anger is uncontrollable.

○ I have a right to express my anger however I want.

○ _____

○ _____

○ _____

○ _____

Part II:

Next to each statement write who you think that "lesson" came from (Mom, Dad, Grandma, Uncle, TV, etc.).

○ Only jerks like my _____ get angry and express their anger.   _____

○ Expressing your anger makes people hate you.   _____

○ You won't have friends if you express your anger.   _____

○ Anger is dangerous.   _____

❍ Feeling angry makes me a bad person.   _____

❍ If I allow myself to feel angry I will hurt someone.   _____

❍ Anger is uncontrollable.   _____

❍ I have a right to express my anger however I want.   _____

❍ _____   _____

❍ _____   _____

❍ _____   _____

❍ _____   _____

Part III:

For each statement, ask yourself: Is this (a) completely true, (b) partially true, (c) untrue?

____ Only jerks like my _____ get angry
and express their anger.   a) completely true   b) partially true   c) untrue

____ Expressing your anger makes people hate you.   a) completely true   b) partially true   c) untrue

____ You won't have friends if you express your anger.   a) completely true   b) partially true   c) untrue

____ Anger is dangerous.   a) completely true   b) partially true   c) untrue

____ Feeling angry makes me a bad person.   a) completely true   b) partially true   c) untrue

____ If I allow myself to feel angry I will hurt someone.   a) completely true   b) partially true   c) untrue

____ Anger is uncontrollable.   a) completely true   b) partially true   c) untrue

____ I have a right to express my anger however I want.   a) completely true   b) partially true   c) untrue

____ _____   a) completely true   b) partially true   c) untrue

____ _____   a) completely true   b) partially true   c) untrue

____ _____   a) completely true   b) partially true   c) untrue

____ _____   a) completely true   b) partially true   c) untrue

Part IV:

This is your opportunity to transform any rigidity you have around this belief system, so that you can test other beliefs. Below, contradict the statements you checked in part I. For example, you can change, "Expressing your anger makes people hate you" to "Expressing your anger can improve your relationships." Or "Only jerks like my _____ get angry and express their anger" can become, "Everyone experiences anger, but people express it in healthy and unhealthy ways."

It's quite all right to develop a statement that seems true, but it's also fine to test a statement in order to explore whether it's true or not. You don't have to believe or agree with your new statements. Just by writing something different from your original belief you can open up to other possibilities for truth.

Picasso-rama

Get some crayons, markers or colored pencils. Sit in a chair and think about a situation at work that makes you angry (or any other situation in your life that makes you angry). Close your eyes and allow your body to relax. Notice your breath as you breathe in and out.

Allow a picture to form in your mind's eye of this situation. It can be a literal representation of the situation, or something more abstract like a symbol. When you are ready, open your eyes and draw this picture or symbol. Title the picture "Anger."

Now think of someone in your life who seems to handle anger well, perhaps a mentor or elder. Perhaps the person is able to express anger in a healthy manner without hurting himself or others. Or perhaps you've seen this person set a clear boundary, get her needs met or right someone's wrong in a way you admired.

Close your eyes again and imagine yourself standing face to face with this wise mentor. Ask him/her to help you with your situation, in a way that does not harm others.

What does your mentor do or say? Is there a new picture or symbol that forms? Draw the new picture and title it, "Another Look at Anger."

MAD PAD

ANGER CANNOT BE
DISHONEST.
— *George R. Bach*

OUT BEYOND IDEAS OF RIGHT DOING
AND WRONG DOING THERE IS A FIELD.
I WILL MEET YOU THERE.

— *Rumi*

CHAPTER 10

THE BEAT GOES ON:
The Practice of Forgiveness

When we hold on to anger and resentment, we hurt ourselves. We suffer, and those around us suffer. When we forgive, we break the chain of unhealthy anger and resentment that has been binding us. We open up to the possibility of a brighter and more joyful future.

In this chapter, we explore why one forgives—the effects of both resentment and forgiveness—and describe the many benefits of healthy forgiveness. You can use this chapter as a road map in learning how to:

- Open up to the possibility of forgiveness
- Recognize when you're ready, rather than trying to force it
- Take responsibility for your experience
- Heal the past

THE WHAT AND WHY OF FORGIVENESS

Wherefore Art Thou Mario?

Mario remembers every person who's done him wrong. He doesn't shop at the butcher's down the road because the butcher's son once shorted him several dollars. He doesn't say hello to his next-door neighbor, Mrs. Palmieri, because her dog steals his newspaper. Ever since his son and daughter-in-law left the Catholic Church, he has refused to visit them.

Because Jessica questioned the business ethics of her sister's fiancé she wasn't invited to the wedding two years ago. Jessica relives the incident on a regular basis with her friends.

Amina is a pressure cooker inside: She's angry that her coworker, Phil, a college buddy of her boss, took all the credit for a project she developed, getting the promotion she deserved. She's mad at herself for feeling powerless to change the situation, and she's furious with the company environment that allows such blatant favoritism to exist.

Forgive for Good

So, who really suffers from all this unhealed anger and resentment?

Mario misses the jovial atmosphere of the butcher's and neighborly chats with Mrs. Palmieri. His resentment hurts his health: Whenever he thinks of his son and daughter-in-law his blood pressure soars.

Jessica longs for the closeness she once had with Erica. Her friends find her "a real downer" and several avoid her.

Amina is unhappy all the time. Her work has become lackadaisical, and she comes home too depressed to enjoy herself.

Holding on to anger and distress is hurting each of them. Resentment can affect health, happiness, spiritual life, effectiveness and the amount of pain in one's life.

In *Forgive For Good,* Fred Luskin, researcher and director of the Stanford University Forgiveness Project, points out many scientifically proven benefits from a practice of healthy forgiving. These include fewer health problems, less stress and feeling better psychologically and emotionally. (Luskin, 2002)

Whose Right Is It Anyway?

Are Mario, Jessica and Amina entitled to feel angry? Of course. And it's human for them to hold on to their angry feelings. One reason people cling to anger and resentment is because they fear that letting go means the person who hurt them "got away with it." We also hold on to anger because we believe we can't trust ourselves to protect ourselves without anger. We can't trust others until we know that we can protect ourselves.

In addressing these concerns, it is helpful to understand that there's a difference between healthy and unhealthy forgiveness. According to author William Defoore, *healthy forgiveness*

- is *not* approval
- does *not* let anyone off the hook
- is *not* the same as absolution—we cannot absolve anyone from being responsible for their actions

We can't always insure that justice will be served. We don't always end up with everything we want; people sometimes take things from us. Forgiveness doesn't restore our world to a perfect state. Healthy forgiveness

- *does* mean that the perpetrator is still accountable for his or her actions

- *can* include fair, appropriate consequences for the perpetrator
- *does* mean letting go of toxic judgments and resentments
- *does* mean acknowledging that you have the power to heal your wounds
- *does* mean being at peace with yourself and accepting what you do have, instead of being hurt by what you don't

Healthy forgiveness and healthy anger have much in common. Both involve taking responsibility for our own actions and our own experience. Both mean letting go of the role of victim. Both can lead to greater health and happiness for ourselves; both can foster deeper communication and intimacy with others.

Here Comes the Sun

Sometimes it's hard to think about forgiveness. Maybe you're not ready to forgive yet. Forgiveness is a process that happens in its own time. It's important not to rush yourself. Forgiveness comes after the tears not before. You may well need to grieve and even to "find yourself" before you can forgive a major trespass. After you have allowed yourself to feel the pain from the past, you might feel the need to forgive or even to reconcile.

It is hard to forgive when you're having difficulty separating the act from the actor. Emotional abuse is unforgivable yet you may be able to forgive the abuser. If you learn that an abusive aunt, who called you names throughout your life, is dying, you may find yourself feeling that you want to reconnect with her. This doesn't mean the name-calling was okay. It means you may want to have the opportunity to liberate yourself from years of resentment.

It's one thing to talk about forgiving a friend who didn't invite you to a party but quite another to consider forgiving someone who was unkind to you throughout your childhood. Personal forgiveness acknowledges that we all are imperfect and at times hurt each other. In order to heal, we may need to learn how to let go of resentments.

TAKING RESPONSIBILITY FOR YOUR OWN EXPERIENCE

It's My Party, and I'll Cry if I Want To

Antwone discovered that his wife Keesha was having an affair with Dan, her coworker. He had always considered Dan a friend. Distraught and furious, he demanded that she move out and threatened to divorce her. After they both had cooled off, they began meeting for coffee and Antwone started to understand what had driven Keesha into Dan's arms.

Antwone was a new associate in a huge law firm, working eighty hours a week in the hope of making partner. Seldom home until late at night, he neglected Keesha during a time when she had had to get a breast lump biopsied. Keesha felt hurt and rejected. She decided to take a hard look at why she chose to have an affair with Dan instead of confronting her husband with her unhappiness and making an effort to work things out. Did she need to be validated by someone else's admiration? Did she crave the excitement of an illicit romance?

Antwone and Keesha began to understand how they had become alienated from each other, and each began to consider individual responsibility for the valley they faced. They decided to try counseling instead of divorce. Keesha agreed to sever all ties with her lover, even though it meant transferring to a different department at work. She moved back in with Antwone and sought her own individual therapy as well as couples counseling with Antwone. Antwone joined a smaller, though less prestigious, law firm in order to spend more evenings at home. A year later, they were rebuilding trust. Despite occasional flare-ups of angry and hurt feelings they remained committed to putting the pain and anger of the past behind them.

Antwone and Keesha each took responsibility for their roles in their troubled marriage. Both were willing to take steps to act accountably toward the other. Through their willingness to make difficult changes, they accepted that their actions involved consequences—neither one stayed in the victim role. They came to understand that while forgiving doesn't mean forgetting, healthy forgiveness, like healthy anger, is a process that can bring problems to light so that they can be addressed. While Keesha sometimes misses the excitement of a wildly passionate liaison and Antwone the chance to be a big player in a major firm, they both realize they have gained much more than they've lost and learned to appreciate their love and marriage.

Poor, Poor Pitiful Me

Practicing healthy forgiveness means accepting the very difficult truth that on some level we're responsible for our experiences. We don't necessarily create those experiences, but we can control, to a large extent, how we respond to them and how we allow them to affect our lives. Being stuck in unhealthy anger means, in part, refusing to give up being the victim. Healthy forgiveness means letting go of that role and taking responsibility for our own healing.

Being a victim can sometimes feel like a very safe place. For some people, it means being "innocent" and not responsible for healing that needs to happen. For others, it can mean the right to sit in judgment. Being a victim is ultimately a powerless position. It gives the perpetrator all the power because your happiness is dependent on someone else's action. Healthy forgiveness does not mean absolution, but it means accepting that you have the power to heal your wounds if you're willing.

Buried Treasure

The idea of forgiveness might bring a specific incident to mind. Or perhaps you're carrying around a load of unresolved resentment from things that happened in the past. Take an honest inventory about the people and events in your life that might be candidates for forgiveness. Whether it's a single incident or an internal smorgasbord of grievances, holding on can rob you of energy, happiness and focus.

Consider the following questions:

• Are there people in my life who I feel have wronged me (a parent, teacher, boss, sibling, friend)?
• Do I spend time reliving hurtful events in my mind?
• Are there unresolved frustrations in my life?
• Do I continually revisit past injustices?
• Do I avoid certain people, because of what they've done to me?
• Do I feel powerless when I think of certain people, groups or institutions?

If you answered yes to any of these, perhaps you harbor some resentment, creating a great opportunity for improving your life as you heal. Can you let go of any incident that this list has brought to mind? Can you think of actions you could take that would make it easier to let go?

One Flight Up

Larry and Mary lived in the same apartment building in San Francisco. The building consisted of two one-bedroom apartments and one studio. A "power" couple, who worked long hours and kept to themselves, occupied the ground floor one-bedroom. Larry lived in the studio directly above Mary's apartment. Because they were both single and shared a staircase and a love of Bette Midler movies, they became fast friends—until one day, when Larry stopped speaking to her.

Mary was completely baffled. Was it something she said, or did? Was it something she didn't say or didn't do? She couldn't come up with anything. A week later, she asked Larry what was going on. Larry snapped back: "I thought we were so close. And then I see THAT!" He pointed to a sign on the building that indicated a one-bedroom apartment for rent. "You didn't even have the courtesy to inform me you were moving out!" "I'm not moving, you idiot," Mary countered, "Debbie and Phil are! If I were, of course I'd have told you!" Larry grimaced sheepishly and offered to make Mary one of his fabulous cappuccinos. The story became part of their history, and they often laughed about it. Larry also admitted to Mary that he felt insecure about his relationships. Mary assured him of her commitment to their friendship; their conversation ultimately led Larry to patch things up with another friend he had rejected in a similar fashion.

The moral of this story is that sometimes we get things wrong. We misinterpret actions, and might at times project our fears onto situations that don't warrant them. If you feel resentful, injured or betrayed by someone, ask yourself if you are reading the facts correctly. Is it possible that the person acted without meaning to hurt you or even that you have misconstrued what actually occurred? The easiest circumstances for forgiveness are those where none is required.

PRACTICING FORGIVENESS

Talking Turkey

Dale and Suzanne had been close friends for a decade. Suzanne's family life was difficult: her sister had been killed by a drunk driver and her parents reacted by clinging together in a way that excluded her. The lonely, secretive Suzanne had never married and seemed to have few friends, and it was, in part, her air of tragedy that drew Dale to her.

When Suzanne's mother's Alzheimer's worsened, her father settled his wife into a nursing home. Two days later he committed suicide. As Dale helped her friend with the funeral arrangements, she noticed that Suzanne seemed very protective of her father. When one of Suzanne's cousins expressed anger at the suicide, Suzanne furiously came to her father's defense.

Five years later the inevitable happened: Suzanne's mother, who had been in a vegetative state for months, finally died. Dale volunteered to help Suzanne prepare for the at-home funeral service.

When Dale arrived, she found Suzanne alone in a filthy house, trying to move her piano out of the living room where the service would be held. "Why not arrange the chairs around the piano?" Dale recommended. "Don't tell me what to do!" Suzanne shouted.

Suzanne proceeded to criticize everything Dale suggested or did. The strain culminated when it was time to prepare a turkey. Dale explained, "I think it would be easier to make a simple roast turkey that we can slice for sandwiches and nix the gravy and stuffing. Anyway, we've got hours of work ahead of us."

Suzanne was livid. "I intend to stuff the turkey and make gravy. You don't know what you're talking about." Dale gritted her teeth, told herself that Suzanne was suffering from loss and grief, and proceeded to help her clean the house. The turkey never got stuffed: Suzanne had no ingredients for stuffing. When a neighbor arrived and suggested that the piano stay put and the chairs be arranged around it, Suzanne agreed.

Although Dale and her husband, Rick, arrived at Suzanne's early the next day to help, Suzanne pointedly ignored them. For the service Suzanne handed each guest a poem to read aloud, blatantly skipping Dale and Rick. Then Suzanne announced that her friend Tisha would manage the kitchen and she would like everyone else to stay out, despite having asked Dale to handle the food the day before. Dale whispered to Rick, "I can't deal with being treated like this any longer. I need to get out of here." They slipped away after the cemetery service.

That evening, she and Rick talked about what happened. "I believe that Suzanne has suppressed a huge amount of rage about her father and the other tragic events in her family," Dale said. "I think that when she lost her mother, those feelings came up but she couldn't handle them. She projected them onto the person who was closest and safest, and that, unfortunately, was me. But still I can't excuse the horrible way she treated me!"

Six months later, Dale still found it difficult to forgive Suzanne for her abusive behavior. "I know I should," she said to herself. "Maybe I'll just do it—call Suzanne and tell her I forgive her." However, the conversation didn't go as planned. Suzanne was defensive and Dale didn't get what she secretly wanted: an admission from Suzanne that what she had done was wrong. "That day at my house you were argumentative and obstinate," Suzanne spoke heatedly. "I had every right to act as I did, and I have nothing to apologize for." That night Dale found herself shaking with fury. She said bitterly to Rick, "I can't believe I wasted ten years of friendship on her. I will never speak to her again."

Breaking the Chain

Both healthy anger and healthy forgiveness have the purpose of bringing about positive change. However, when you try to force yourself to forgive before you're ready, you might end up in the mire of unhealthy forgiveness. Like unhealthy anger, this kind of "forgiveness" can be destructive. If you try to forgive before you're ready to really let go, if you go about it dishonestly or with ulterior motives, or if you demand consequences that are inappropriate, you'll gain none of the benefits and might find yourself more deeply mired in anger than before.

Healthy forgiveness doesn't just happen—it's a conscious choice. Like quitting smoking: First you have to want to or you'll never succeed. So what does it take to forgive? The following are the elements of forgiveness. There may be some overlap between steps. Follow your own heart and intuition about what works best for you.

Timing: understanding that healthy forgiveness can't be forced—it happens when you're ready
Responsibility: realizing your power to create happiness for yourself and being willing to let go of the role of victim
Healing: taking steps to start healing your own wounds
Compassion: acknowledging that the person who hurt you might also be suffering

Timing

How do you get ready to forgive? As we've said, forgiveness is a decision, an intention, or for some, it might come up automatically. Choosing to forgive means that you are taking a leap of faith: faith that you don't have to remain a victim and that it's possible to live in the light of love and compassion rather than in the darkness of unresolved anger and bitterness. Like any act of faith, all you are required to do is choose to be on the path. As long as you don't abandon the path, it will open before you. And like any true path, the journey is what counts, not the destination.

Responsibility

Is something holding you back? Consider these questions:

- Do I feel that certain people have deprived me of what I deserve?
- Do I condemn or wish harm to certain people for what they've done to me?
- Do I tell myself I'm better than another person because I would *never* act the way he/she does?
- Do I believe that my suffering makes me superior?

If you answered yes to any of these, you might consider thinking about what it means to you to be a victim. What benefits do you get from the victim role? If you let go of being a victim, what do you think you might lose? You may want to make notes about these questions on your *Mad Pad*.

Compassion

We've all heard the saying about walking a mile in another's moccasins. Compassion means recognizing what we all have in common rather than what separates us. Reflect on these questions:

- Can I think of any reason why the person who hurt me might have acted as he/she did?
- Is it possible that the person hurt me without meaning to? If so, does this knowledge have any effect on my angry feelings?
- Have I ever committed a similar grievance against another person? If so, what was my reason?
- Do I know anything of the perpetrator's past history that might help me better understand—without justifying—his/her behavior? (However, don't consider this question until you've honored your own feelings of pain and anger.)

Use your answers to these questions to help you gain a measure of compassion for the person who hurt you. Most of the time, people do act for a reason, even if that reason is deeply flawed. Remember, compassion is not absolution. The person who hurt you—the person you are trying to forgive—is accountable for his/her actions. Sometimes you'll be in a position to ask for appropriate consequences—sometimes not. However, if you can view the situation with compassion, you will be in the very powerful position of creating a context of love that can heal you both. You might never completely understand why the person did what he or she did, but love and compassion, as most great spiritual texts assert, offer a truth that is far greater than understanding.

Sticks and Stones

Bette's grandfather would never ask forgiveness for the beatings he gave her: He was dead. While he was responsible for terrible abuse, Bette finally decided she was responsible for how it affected her now. She was twenty-seven, and her life was a mess. She couldn't hold onto a decent job, seemed to have a knack for choosing the worst possible men, and realized her drinking had gotten out of control. She recognized that most of her troubles stemmed from her childhood abuse. For six years, with the help of a therapist, Bette worked through her anger and painful memories. She finally came to understand that she no longer wanted to be a victim: If she continued to hate her grandfather and feel helpless about her trauma and anger, she would remain stuck. She chose instead to see herself as someone with strength and power—she refused to let the anguish of her early experience define who she was.

Samuel was shamed throughout his childhood by the raging insults of his alcoholic mother. Early in healing, Samuel felt rage at her for the demeaning names she'd hurled at him. The more he healed, the less energy he focused on his mother and the more he directed his energy to the little boy inside him who'd been so helpless. He nurtured this part of himself and began to feel more whole. His mother was no longer at the center of his healing—he was.

The Healing Journey

The healing path is different for every individual, but it will probably include:

- Acknowledging your pain
- Feeling your feelings
- Learning to seek support when triggered and being responsible for those triggers
- Exploring the cause of your pain through meditation, therapy, or some other internal work
- Allowing the experience to change or shift in some way: in other words, allowing for the possibility of transformation

It can be helpful to acknowledge your wound or pain in writing. Healing can be hard work. It can take a day or two for something small, but the stuff of childhood might take decades to heal. It's a process. And forgiveness can happen somewhere during the process, or throughout the process.

In order to forgive a major trespass, you may need to look for assistance with your own healing. Share your experience with a wise friend, spiritual teacher or mentor. You might want to consult a professional therapist or counselor, especially if you are working with a big issue. Benefits include the therapist's professional training, experience and insight, and having someone act as a witness for you, which is an important aspect of healing. In addition, use the *Anger-obics*SM exercises in this book to help in your healing process and read other useful books on healing [see resources section for our suggestions].

You may want to use prayer or ritual to prepare yourself. You can call upon God, Goddess, Allah, Buddha, Jesus, Great Spirit, Nature, your own spirit guides: however you view those resources in the universe which are available to you for healing. You may simply say, "Creator, please help me forgive _____ for _____," or recite the Christian prayer that asks for help to "forgive those who trespass against us."

WHEN YOU NEED TO FORGIVE YOURSELF

The Long and Winding Road

Sometimes the hardest person to forgive is you. When your words or actions have injured another, the result can be overwhelming feelings of guilt and remorse. How do you practice healthy forgiveness when the recipient is yourself?

The principles of healthy forgiveness remain the same, whether you're striving to forgive another or yourself. The first thing to remember is that forgiving yourself doesn't mean that you're letting yourself off the hook. Depending on the gravity of what you did, healthy forgiveness toward yourself can involve:

- Acknowledging that you were wrong and asking forgiveness of the person you hurt
- Making appropriate reparations when possible
- Honestly examining your injurious behavior and making the commitment to change—this can be as simple as deciding not to gossip anymore, or as life-altering as admitting that you're an alcoholic and entering a program
- Recognizing that we are all imperfect, that we make mistakes—some of them doozies—and that it's okay to let go and move on if you've done all you can to address the situation

Sometimes you're not going to be able to make amends to the person you harmed. The person might be physically distant, otherwise unavailable, not willing to forgive at this time, or even dead. In those cases, do the best you can to take responsibility for what you did and to make amends. For example, if you were unkind to a troubled friend who went on to commit suicide, or stopped speaking to a family member who then suddenly died, perhaps you could determine to be more understanding in the future; or, in the memory of your lost friend, volunteer at a crisis hotline.

Because suicide is such a painful and guilt-provoking experience for those left behind, it can be helpful for a family, individual or group of individuals to process the experience through letter-writing. The letter can say everything you would have liked to say before the person died. You can include all the things you wanted to do and didn't, any apologies you would like to make or anger you feel about the act of suicide (suicide is like someone permanently hanging up on you; your guilt can sometimes block your anger and keep you stuck). The letter can then be burned or buried. While writing and burning/burying the letter, it is important to have the support of a friend, family member or counselor. You may choose to read the letter to a support person, or talk about your feelings when writing the letter, before burning or burying it.

Unresolved guilt and regret, like unhealthy anger, can poison your life if you let it. In the example above, being accountable for your actions doesn't mean that you take responsibility for your friend's decision to commit suicide. It's normal and healthy to feel bad if you've done something wrong: It can motivate you to try to put things right. It's neither normal nor healthy to inappropriately take on the actions of others and to hold on to remorse. Treat yourself with compassion.

If you find that you're feeling shame or guilt over situations that were beyond your control, you may want to explore with a therapist or other trusted counselor the possibility that you're responding to something that happened in your childhood. Children often feel responsible for situations such as a parent's illness, drinking or abuse.

For example, Felice, whose mother suffered from undiagnosed bipolar disease, grew up convinced that if she had only been a "perfect" child her mother wouldn't have been ill. As an adult, Felice frequently felt guilty about situations she hadn't caused and couldn't control. When she did do something about which she had a legitimate reason to feel remorseful, her feelings of guilt were wildly out of proportion: Instead of being able to make appropriate amends and forgive herself, she was paralyzed by shame. If this sounds like a familiar pattern in your own life, you may greatly benefit from the guidance of a therapist to discover and free yourself from those irrational childhood beliefs.

Anger-obics^{SM}: Move Your Body, Shift Your Mind

Let Freedom Ring

What are some of the benefits you would like to experience from letting go of unhealthy anger and resentment?

○ Feel powerful and in control, rather than feeling controlled by others.

○ Increase my energy.

○ Experience more joy.

○ Have better relationships with others.

○ Be more present with myself and others.

○ Improve creativity.

○ Other _____.

○ Other _____.

○ Other _____.

○ Other _____.

○ Other _____.

○ Other _____.

○ Other _____.

Hula Hips

1. Stand with your feet hip-width apart and your knees slightly bent.

2. Put your hands on your hips and move your hips in a circular motion.

3. As you move your hips, remember something that made you angry or imagine one of the angry situations in appendix C.

4. Imagine that as you move your hips you become taller and stronger. Your voice becomes louder. See yourself as big as a mountain. Enjoy this feeling of being tall and big.

5. Now wind your hips in the opposite direction. As you unwind, imagine that any unhealthy anger and resentment is releasing from your body, like a rapidly flowing river.

6. As the anger releases, is there something you want to say?

Poem Blessing*

1. Think of someone you love and read this poem aloud as you think about him/her, imagining that you are saying these words to the person:

> *You were once a small baby, crying and asking for your mother's milk.*
> *You were once a child, seeking love, approval and joy.*
> *You grew into an adult, still needing love, still hoping to be understood.*
> *Now I look at you, see the aching in your heart.*
> *Perhaps our differences are not as deep as I imagined.*
> *May you find love and understanding.*
> *May you be blessed with the light of the sun, the twinkling of stars, the joy of a sparrow's song.*

2. How did it feel to read this poem to someone you love?

_____

_____

_____

*"Poem Blessing" was inspired by a meditation/sermon by Unitarian Universalist minister Tricia Newport Hart. The poem was written by Lisa Tener.

3. Now think of someone with whom you are angry. Read the poem again imagining you are saying the words to this person.

_____

_____

4. How did it feel to read the poem to the person with whom you felt angry? Write about the experience below.

_____

_____

You may wish to tape yourself saying the poem so that you can close your eyes and focus on the person (or have someone read you the poem).

Yoga Mudra

As the title suggests, this exercise is derived from yoga. The quiet awareness one brings to yoga is often an acquired skill. Be patient with yourself if this feels new to you. If you return to this exercise over time, it becomes easier and more potent. Think of an incident for which you would like to forgive yourself or someone else.

Sit in a kneeling position and allow your buttocks to sink down onto your heels. You may wish to place a pillow between your calves and thighs to make this more comfortable.

Now bring your hands to your heart in a prayer position and inhale as you place your awareness at your heart center. Think of something that makes you angry with yourself (or another person). Choose to work on forgiving yourself (or the person) and let go of this anger or self-blame.

Now place your hands on the floor in front of your knees, shoulder-length apart, and place your forehead on the floor. As you bend down to place your head on the floor, exhale, imagining that with the breath, you are releasing the anger.

Stay in this position for a minute or two and with each breath out feel yourself release the anger or blame even more. Relax into the floor, allowing your muscles to relax as the floor supports you.

When you are ready, slowly come up to the kneeling position, imagining that you are stacking your vertebrae one on top of the other. Bring your hands to your heart again and, as you breathe in, allow yourself to feel a sense of peace within. As you breathe out, allow that sense of peace to be directed outward toward the world.

MAD PAD

_____

_____

_____

_____

_____

_____

FORGIVENESS DOES NOT CHANGE
THE PAST, BUT IT DOES
ENLARGE THE FUTURE.

— *Paul Boese*

_____

_____

_____

THE WEAK CAN NEVER FORGIVE.
FORGIVENESS IS THE ATTRIBUTE OF
THE STRONG.

— *Mahatma Gandhi*

CHAPTER 11

TAKE ME TO THE RIVER:
Anger, Spirituality and Purpose

WHEN YOU'RE ANGRY AT GOD* OR THE UNIVERSE

This chapter enlarges our exploration of anger to include anger's spiritual dimension. For most people, the term *spirituality* implies some form of belief in a reality that encompasses and transcends the limitations of our lives. In this chapter, we expand on our exploration of healthy anger to include how anger can be an intrinsic part of spirituality, even in the face of loss and suffering. We look at how unhealthy anger, taken to the extreme, can turn into hatred and iniquity, just as healthy anger at its most noble can be heroic. Finally, we see how the flame that burns in the heart of anger can clarify our purpose in the world.

Many Rivers to Cross

Ingrid lost both of her parents in a car accident when she was only thirteen. Until college she lived on an isolated farm with an elderly aunt who was conscientious but emotionally distant. In her junior year, she

---

*Throughout this chapter, we use several terms for Divinity, but please substitute whatever term is comfortable for you: Higher Power, God, Goddess, Great Spirit, Holy Spirit, Jesus, Nature, Allah, Buddha, Creator or any other.

met Jurgen, and they fell deeply in love. Finally, Ingrid thought, "I've found someone who truly cherishes me. I don't have to be lonely any more!" Jurgen proposed to Ingrid the week before they graduated. They planned a late fall wedding and a honeymoon trip to Hawaii. However, in July Jurgen began suffering from intense headaches and the vision in one eye began to blur. He was diagnosed with a malignant, inoperable brain tumor. Instead of a November wedding, Ingrid found herself planning Jurgen's memorial service. "I don't understand why all this has happened to me!" she cried to a friend. "I'm starting to feel like I hate God." In the three years since Jurgen's death, Ingrid has remained bitter and closed to any possibility of happiness. "Why should I hope for anything?" she shrugs. "God will just take it away."

It is difficult not to blame the Creator or the universe for the worst pains we have experienced, particularly those in childhood, and for the suffering we see around us. Who else can we blame, ultimately, for the existence of child abuse, sexual abuse, murders, neglect, unfit parents, wars, famines and other horrors?

It's a Mad, Mad, Mad, Mad World

Nobody can adequately explain the existence, in our world, of pain and misery. It's especially difficult to understand when innocent people and creatures suffer. Sometimes the source of the pain is a specific person: a man who batters his wife, a woman who neglects her child, a burglar who shoots a clerk, a couple who torture their dog, or a manufacturer who pollutes a river. In those cases, we have a target for our anger. Sometimes we can even change the situation.

All too often the suffering seems randomly inflicted by an inhuman hand, and there's nothing we can do. We watch helplessly as desperately poor people in Bangladesh lose their remaining possessions in a flood. We see devastating images of people and lands ravaged by war and famine. Many people live lives that are burdened with financial and other woes. We review our own lives and find many instances when life treated us unfairly or cruelly. The scale of suffering seems vast and endless—how can a "just" Creator allow for it?

Amazing Grace

If our suffering is the result of someone's actions—an abusive parent, an unfaithful lover, a demeaning boss—we have the means to heal those wounds through a practice of healthy forgiveness [as discussed in chapter 10].

Sometimes our tribulations aren't the result of any specific person's actions. The anger we feel at life's injustices can seem purposeless and futile. But is it? And is there any way to apply the principles of healthy forgiveness to those situations where it seems as if the universe itself is to blame?

The primary thing to remember is that the process of forgiveness, whether it's about your alcoholic mother or a heartless world, is an act of grace. When you believe that forgiveness is the right thing to do and try to accomplish it, it means that you have moved through your pain and then can take responsibility for your experience and your choices at the deepest level. It also means that you acknowledge compassion as the highest wisdom.

You can acknowledge that you might never understand why suffering exists. Letting go of resentment at God doesn't mean that you stop noticing what's around you or stop caring. It doesn't mean that you sanction suffering or give up trying to do something about it. But letting go can allow you to reconnect with the love, beauty and joy that life also offers, and restore you to a place of gratitude for the gifts in your life.

Here are some strategies:

- Take a moment to "count your blessings." Think of small, everyday pleasures and gifts—a caring phone call from a friend, a cup of chowder on a cold day, a spring field of wildflowers, a coworker telling you "job well done." Even if it feels like the universe has treated you badly, you might be surprised to discover how much abundance your life contains.
- If your misfortune is personal, such as suffering a life-altering injury in an accident, can you find any blessing in what happened? People in such circumstances often talk about how what seemed so tragic ended up resulting in greater serenity, a better sense of what's important, more profound relationships, a healthier lifestyle or a deeper certainty of being connected to life.
- Ask yourself if there is something you can do, even something small, to help alleviate someone else's suffering. Maybe you could volunteer your time at an animal shelter, or "adopt" a child through a monthly contribution to an agency such as Save the Children. Look for opportunities every day to demonstrate kindness.
- Ask yourself if you've gained anything positive from your experience, such as learning how to eat healthier or better manage stress.
- Let your anger motivate you to speak out or act concerning issues you care about, such as organizing a food drive at your local place of worship.
- Pray, meditate, or ask for the wisdom to let go. There are many wonderful books on this subject by great spiritual teachers; we've included some of them in the resources section. If you're so inclined, create a ritual about your decision to let go. You might write about your anger on a piece of paper, then burn or bury it.
- Talk with a wise friend, teacher or therapist. Such people can help you gain insight into your own needs and processes, and they can act as witnesses to your healing.

INCORPORATING ANGER WORK INTO A SPIRITUAL PRACTICE

Stairway to Heaven

Most of us yearn for a connection to something larger than ourselves. We want to live in a context that will help illuminate our own struggles and fears, and guide our life's journey. A spiritual practice, whether grounded in an organized religion or based on a private sense of the sacred, is, for many, as necessary for living as are food and companionship.

Often we get the message that anger and the spiritual are mutually exclusive. We're told that the only proper way to approach the Creator is through love, joy, praise and humility. However, if spirituality means connection with the Divine in life, then how can we fully connect unless we do so with our whole selves?

The underlying message of this book is that healthy anger in all its components—among them insight, problem-solving, healthy forgiveness—can be a positive force for good, in our lives and in the world. Healthy anger can help us communicate more clearly, deepen our relationships, challenge injustices, and enhance clarity and creativity. To deny healthy anger its rightful place in our lives is to deny a part of who we are.

"When my mother was diagnosed with lung cancer," Donatella relates, "she was angry at everyone: herself for smoking for forty years, the tobacco industry for promoting a poisonous and addictive product, my father for not taking away her cigarettes, me for I'm not sure what—growing up and leaving home and not being around when she got sick. As her cancer advanced, she tried every kind of conventional and unconventional treatment. Nothing seemed to work and her pain and discomfort got worse. She became negative about her family, society, and whatever forces in nature had made her sick. She told everyone who would listen what a total waste her life had been. Finally she began seeing a spiritual teacher as well as a therapist and began to explore why she was so angry. The therapist helped her uncover patterns and disappointments in her past, and her teacher helped her gain perspective on what she could accomplish despite her condition. As a result, she turned her inward anger outward, and as she continued treatment she began volunteering for an organization that works to end teenage smoking. She even testified against 'big tobacco' for a congressional committee! Today, her cancer is still with her, but she's taken control of managing her pain, which is something she hadn't done before. She's peaceful and accepts her life as it is."

Beacons of Hope

In the previous chapter, we focused on the kind of forgiveness we can practice, to varying degrees, throughout our lives. Another level of forgiveness has more to do with fundamental questions of morality, such as those provoked by terrorists and other people whose actions can cause great harm in the world. The fact that those terrible deeds are not directed at any particular person can make it all the more difficult to contemplate forgiveness.

Some of the most inspiring human stories have as their source unforgivable acts. Former slave Sojourner Truth, who transformed her experience into poetry; Nelson Mandela, who confronted apartheid and changed a nation; Reginald Denny, who was dragged from his truck and brutally beaten during the South Central LA riots, only to speak out for compassion for his assailants.

Does Your Dogma Bite? Fanaticism and Terrorism

The *New Shorter Oxford Dictionary* defines a fanatic as "a person filled with excessive and mistaken enthusiasm." Fanatics usually belong to a particular religious or political group and are characterized by a rigid and unyielding belief that only they are in possession of the truth. All religions and spiritual practices have great teachers, and their message is consistent: We can only save the world through love, compassion, and forgiveness, the very antitheses of fanaticism. If you're dealing with a fanatic, try not to buy into his or her rigid and unyielding perspective. Instead, your empathy and forbearance might serve as a model of healing that is more powerful than the fanatic's intolerance.

Terrorism is fanaticism at its most devastating level. Most terrorists are religious or political fanatics; terrorism, whatever the source, is a toxic plant with roots that go deep into the darkest recesses of human nature. Terrorism can grow in various climates: hatred, powerlessness, hopelessness, childhood abuse, psychiatric conditions such as monomania, as well as indoctrination and an excessive sense of entitlement. As we know from the events of September 11, terrorists come from all walks of life—several of the hijackers grew up in wealthy and privileged families—but one thing they share is the most destructive form of unhealthy anger.

One of the great dangers of terrorism is that its victims can become poisoned by hatred and revenge. Ultimately these forms of response only serve to make the wounds of terrorism harder to cure. Try to remember that evil deeds are not necessarily done by evil people. Some terrorists might be more desperate or manipulated than truly wicked—condemn the deed but not the doer. Feel healthy anger and allow yourself to grieve. Demand justice but have compassion, if you can, for the perpetrators. Focus on your own healing. Here we offer one approach, through ceremony and ritual, which might help you deal with the wrenching impact on your spirit and soul of the presence of fanaticism and terrorism in our world.

Ceremony and ritual allow us the expression of strong emotions—grief, joy, anger and gratitude. Rituals help us feel less alone in times of difficulty by strengthening our sense of community, acknowledging life transitions and rites of passage, and providing a sense of belonging. The following example is the account of a ritual conducted by Jane Middelton-Moz in the aftermath of September 11.

Where Were You When the World Stopped Turning?

Many of the two hundred individuals sat staring straight ahead with their arms folded, their body language saying, "We're all done with our grieving, and we're getting on with our lives." It had been six months since four planes had set off from their respective airports and changed the lives of millions of Americans forever.

Jane selected people from the group to represent the eyes, ears, and voices of the mothers, fathers, grandparents, sons, daughters, aunts and uncles, nephews and nieces who had witnessed the tragic events of September 11. She directed them to seats in front of the large group. Everyone stood as Alan Jackson's "Where Were You When the World Stopped Turning?" began to play in the background. The faces of the group began to change. Tears fell as hands seeking comfort reached out to clasp those of a neighbor. The small group that had been chosen to represent the many gave voice to what was seen, heard and felt on that painful day. A grandmother sobbed as she talked about her feelings the day she held her grandchildren close and watched the towers collapse. A mother wept as she spoke of the children left without parents. A brother sobbed as he talked of lost siblings. One by one, the witnesses gave voice to the overwhelming pain still felt by so many.

When the witnessing was complete, everyone was given paper and the chance to write whatever they wanted that had yet to be given voice. Later they would burn the paper in a fire-burning ceremony outside the auditorium. Some wrote letters to the thousands lost; some wrote angry letters to the terrorists responsible; others to the families left behind; still others, poems and prayers for peace. Many shared their feelings before they burned their letters.

After the burning, Jane placed a box of wooden blocks in the middle of the room. She asked participants what they thought it would take to symbolically rebuild the fallen towers. Those who wished to participate identified the qualities needed for rebuilding, as they placed block upon block to symbolically rebuild the towers. "This block represents love," "this is tolerance," "acceptance of one another," "truth," "spirituality" and so on. As a man placed the last block, a symbolic replica of the Twin Towers stood in the middle of the group. Tears fell again as John Lennon's "Imagine" softly played.

Jane gave each of the two hundred participants a packet of flower seeds. She asked them to think of one thing that they wanted to have grow in their own lives from of the tragedy of September 11 and one thing they were willing to give up to allow their wish to blossom. She invited them, when they returned home, to plant the seeds as symbols of the wishes they wanted to cultivate. She asked everyone to make a commitment that would allow their wishes to grow as they watered their seeds. People chosen to represent the North, South, East and West came to the microphone and shared their wishes and commitments: "I would like our neighborhoods to be safer for our children." "I'm going to give up some of my free time to work with my neighbors to start a 'block watch' in my neighborhood." After all representatives had voiced their dreams and the gifts they were offering to help their dreams grow, participants formed a circle around the room. People circled the room shaking hands, giving and receiving hugs, sharing prayers for peace and crying together, as music from many cultures filled the room.

In your own life, you can create personal or group ceremonies that help you heal angry or resentful "wounds." Some of the elements you may want to include are: finding symbols to express the healing (people to represent the human family, blocks to represent rebuilding the towers); expressing your feelings; taking symbolic action to let go of something (such as burning the papers); taking symbolic action to create change (symbolically rebuilding the towers with special qualities, planting seeds). Singing and dancing can enrich a ceremony, as can prayer.

ANGER AND THE POWER OF PURPOSE

Tell Me a Secret

Anger is a messenger. Anger tells you that something is wrong, that you're being treated badly, that danger lurks. Anger also bears gifts, if you develop the awareness to see them. Anger can bring many skills that help you grow into a person of compassion and commitment. Healthy anger can give you a voice and help sustain the power of your voice in the world.

William Defoore and other anger experts talk about "spiritual warriors," people who practice healthy anger and healthy forgiveness. These people live their lives in a context of love; they refuse to allow circumstances or other people to turn them into victims; they radiate compassion and insight, and by their work and presence make the world a better place. This healthy manifestation of personal power is what defines a spiritual warrior. When you become a spiritual warrior, you accept anger as a teacher, a teacher that can alert you to what is important and what requires a response. You learn to use anger to help reveal your purpose and to give you the energy to achieve it.

Even if your circumstances are such that you fear that expressing your anger might bring retribution, you can still nurture that voice internally. Don't let a repressive political regime, an abusive marriage, an exploitative job situation silence your inner wisdom and the guidance that anger can offer. Let the flame of your healthy anger burn bright; it may illuminate the path to a better tomorrow.

All of Me

The most spiritually effective people in the world have certain characteristics in common. They share qualities of vision, commitment, compassion, diligence and a sense of wholeness. Healthy anger is an intrinsic element in all of those qualities: the eyes, the will, the heart and the energy to accomplish good—from being a loving parent to fighting racism.

Embrace your anger as an essential part of who you are. Listen to its messages and accept its offerings. Practice healthy anger and healthy forgiveness, and become a whole and integrated person who can act with power on whatever stage you choose.

Anger-obics*SM*: Move Your Body, Shift Your Mind

Soul Talk

You may want to first try this exercise thinking of someone with whom you are slightly angry, or someone who is not hugely important in your life. After you have worked with your anger more and become comfortable, you can choose someone with whom you are very angry or someone you are very close to, such as a parent.

Close your eyes and take a breath. You can start with Gratitude Attitude [chapter 2] or the Golden Healing Light Meditation [chapter 3], or just bring your attention to the area of your heart as you breathe. With each breath imagine love and joy entering your heart.

With your eyes still closed, think of someone with whom you are angry. Picture her or just imagine that you are connecting with her essence. Continue to feel a connection to the love energy in your heart.

Now imagine looking into the person's eyes. Imagine that through her eyes you connect with her soul essence. As you are looking into her eyes, ask what message she has for you. "Listen" for her answer with your eyes, your heart and your whole being. The message may come as words, as a physical or emotional sensation, or as a picture or image.

Often, when we connect at a soul level, we receive a purer message than the messages the person normally gives us in day-to-day life. Perhaps you can sense the person's love, or her own fear. This exercise can help provide some understanding and compassion for the person. You may find that, suddenly, whatever "mean" or hurtful thing the person has been doing won't affect you as much.

Write about the message you sense from the person, or draw a picture if you prefer. If you draw a picture, give the picture a title.

Note: The heart of "Soul Talk," looking into the person's eyes and listening/asking for a message, is inspired by Heart-Centered Therapy, developed by Alaya Chikly.

Spiritual Warrior

In yoga, an ancient tradition that includes body postures and movements for increased health and vitality, there are many variations of a posture called "Warrior." The posture helps you to feel strong and powerful, not a warrior who fights wars, but one who is here to instill health and peace. Here is one variation with our words added:

Stand with your legs about three feet apart, toes facing forward. Turn your left foot in slightly. Turn your right foot ninety degrees (a quarter of a circle) so that it faces the right wall. Keeping your left leg straight, bend your right knee so that it is directly over your ankle. You may want to move your left foot back even more, making the space between your legs larger, if that is more comfortable.

Raise your left arm out to the left and your right arm to the right, so that they are pointing to the walls on either side of you. Stretch your arms out to each wall, while keeping your shoulders and the rest of your body relaxed. While keeping your body facing forward, turn your head to the right wall, the same direction your right foot is pointing.

Stand in this position for a few minutes and say, "I am a strong, powerful man (woman). I do not need to use force to make my way in the world. I do not need to yell or say hurtful things. I am not cowed by other people's yelling, posturing or bullying.

"I feel my strong connection to earth below me. I am strengthened by my connection to the sun above. (You can replace the word "sun" with "Spirit," "God," "My Higher Self" or something similar.) My left hand reaches into the past for wisdom and learning. My right hand reaches into the world as I express myself clearly and take actions that are healthy and wise. I am fully alive in the present moment. I claim my place in the world. I positively influence the world around me."

You are the spiritual warrior, a peaceful warrior. You may wish to write here about your experience.

_____

_____

_____

_____

Cell-a-Brate

Follow the "Golden Healing Light" exercise from chapter 1. When you get to the part about feeling the Golden Healing Light in every cell, imagine that there is just one cell that is not filled with light. Imagine that this cell is angry. In your mind's eye, allow an image or symbol to form of this cell. (There are no wrong answers: It doesn't matter what image you get.)

Open your eyes and draw a picture of the image or symbol of the angry cell.

Now close your eyes again and imagine breathing into that angry cell. With each breath, light and love enter the cell and transform the anger. See the image or symbol of the cell become filled with light. Allow a change to take place inside that cell. Now open your eyes and draw a picture of what you imagine the cell to look like after the light has filled it and the anger has transformed.

It can be helpful to have someone read this exercise to you, or you may wish to tape it and play it back for yourself.

Circle of Friends

Imagine that you are gathering a group of powerful, effective people together to help you transform your unhealthy anger patterns. They can include a historical figure, a sports star, loved ones, an unseen guide, a special animal, an angel, God, whomever you would like to imagine helping you. Close your eyes and picture yourself holding hands in this circle of supporters. Imagine that the circle you are all forming by holding hands creates a safe space for you and your anger.

Think about a situation that recently made you angry. If you can't think of one, pick one of the situations in appendix C. As you picture the situation, imagine your anger being contained in a ball of white light. Now imagine the "anger ball" on the floor in front of you. Bend down and pick up the ball. With your whole body throw the anger ball into the center of the circle so that your guides may help you heal the situation in some way. You may even want to say some words asking your guides and helpers for support.

Imagine that your helpers/guides are assisting you with the anger. Do they transform the situation? Help you change your perspective? Transform your anger? Does the anger ball change shape or color? Does something about the situation change? What happens? Is this a surprise? Did you learn anything from this exercise?

When you feel ready, open your eyes and write about your experience or draw a picture of any changes that took place.

MAD PAD

ANGER WILL NEVER DISAPPEAR
SO LONG AS THOUGHTS OF RESENTMENT
ARE CHERISHED IN THE MIND. ANGER WILL
DISAPPEAR JUST AS SOON AS THOUGHTS
OF RESENTMENT ARE FORGOTTEN.

— *Buddha*

ANGER IS A GREAT FORCE.
IF YOU CONTROL IT, IT CAN BE
TRANSMUTED INTO A POWER
WHICH CAN MOVE THE WHOLE WORLD.

— *Sri Swami Sivananda*

1. **Ground Rules:**
- No physical violence
- No name-calling
- No shouting

2. **Time-Outs:**
- Call them when needed
- Take one when the other person calls for them
- Two hours minimum; be in separate rooms; no talking
- Do something to help you to calm down: exercise, *Anger-obics*^SM, a creative activity or meditation
- Don't dwell on rage, avoid binging and steer clear of television or video games

3. **Clear Communication:**
- Active listening
- Take responsibility for your perceptions and reaction
- "When you . . . I feel . . . I need . . ."

4. **Negotiate an agreement**

5. **Follow through**

6. **Reevaluate**

You may wish to photocopy the previous page and keep it somewhere easy to find, such as on the side of your refrigerator, or on the back of a cupboard or closet door. You might consider tucking a copy away in every room of the house!

Greg: I need to take a time-out. Let's talk in a couple of hours.

(They go to separate rooms for two hours and meet back again.)

Greg: When you complain about my mother, I feel stuck in the middle. I need for you to discuss her actions directly with her if they bother you.

Sally: You think I was wrong about your mother.

Greg: No, I just feel stuck in the middle when you complain to me. I need for you to discuss her actions directly with her if they bother you.

Sally: I hear you saying that when I talk about your mom with you, it puts you in the middle. You don't want me to talk to you about it.

Greg: I'd like you to talk to her instead.

Sally: You'd like me to talk directly to her.

Greg: Yes.

Sally: Well, she's your mom, and I feel I need to talk to someone about it first.

Greg: I hear you saying that you want to talk about it. Because she's my mother, you want that to be me.

Sally: Yes.

Greg: I understand your need to talk about it, but when you raise your voice and complain and go on and on I feel angry.

Sally: I hear you say that you feel angry when I yell and complain.

Greg: Yes. And I feel like I'm getting attacked instead of her.

Sally: And you feel like you're being attacked.

Greg: Uh huh. Maybe you could just use the same language with her: "When you . . . I feel . . . I need . . ."

Sally: You're suggesting I use this language with her.

Greg: Yeah.

Sally: I suppose I could try it. If it doesn't work, could I talk to you about it?

Greg: How about you talk about it with her tomorrow when I'm there, too. Then we can problem solve together afterwards if it doesn't work.

Sally: You want me to talk with her about it at lunch tomorrow. If it doesn't work we can talk about it again.

Greg: Yes.

Sally: Okay.

In your Anger-obics^{SM} exercises . . .

- You are crossing the street at a crosswalk and a speeding driver on a car phone almost hits you.
- An aggressive driver pulls out in front of you in traffic and you have to slam on your brakes so as not to hit him.
- Someone cuts in front of you in line at the supermarket.
- You made plans to go to a special event a months ago, making sure your baby-sitter knew that this was an important commitment. The day before the event, she cancels in order to attend a rock concert with her boyfriend.
- Your wife/husband has left clothes and paperwork strewn all over the bedroom and living room floor yet again.
- Your housemate/partner has left dirty dishes in the sink for over twenty-four hours.
- Your friend/sister/cousin doesn't invite you to her wedding!
- Your best friend forgets your birthday.

- Your boss takes credit for work you did.
- Your boss/coworker purposely makes you look badly in front of others.
- Your "friend"/coworker spreads malicious gossip about you.
- Your date doesn't show.
- Your toddler refuses to wear clothing of any kind.
- Your daughter/son won't clean up her/his toys.
- Your children are fighting again.
- A telemarketer calls during dinnertime.

List your own situations here:

_____

_____

_____

_____

_____

_____

_____

REFERENCES AND RESOURCES

Books

Abdullah, Sharif M. *The Power of One: Authentic Leadership in Turbulent Times.* Philadelphia: New Society Publishers, 1995.

Bach, George R. and Wyden, Peter. *The Intimate Enemy: How to Fight Fair in Love and Marriage.* New York: William Morrow and Company, Inc., 1969.

Childre, Doc, Martin, Howard, with Beech, Donna. *The Heartmath Solution: The Institute of HeartMath's Revolutionary Program for Engaging the Power of the Heart's Intelligence.* San Francisco: Harper San Francisco, 1999.

Covey, Stephen R. *The Seven Habits of Highly Effective People: Restoring the Character Ethic.* New York: Simon & Schuster, 1989.

Dalai Lama. *Dzogchen: The Heart Essence of the Great Perfection.* Ithaca, N.Y.: Snow Lion Publications, 2000.

Dayton, Tian. *Trauma and Addiction: Ending the Cycle of Pain Through Emotional Literacy.* Deerfield Beach, Fla.: Health Communications, Inc., 2000.

Enright, Robert D. *Forgiveness Is a Choice: A Step-By-Step Process for Resolving Anger and Restoring Hope.* Washington, D.C.: American Psychological Association, 2001.

Fry, Virginia. *Part of Me Died Too: Stories of Creative Survival Among Bereaved Children and Teenagers.* New York: Dutton Children's Books, 1995.

Garrity, C.,K. Jens, W. Porter, N. Sager, and C.Short-Camilli. *Bully-Proofing Your School.* Logmont, Colo.: Sopris West, 1994.

Grossman, David. *On Killing: The Psychological Cost of Learning to Kill in War and Society.* Boston: Little, Brown and Company, 1995.

Hanh, Thich Nhat. *Anger: Wisdom for Cooling the Flames.* New York: Riverhead Books, 2001.

————. *The Heart of the Buddha's Teaching: Tranforming Suffering into Peace, Joy, and Liberation.* New York: Broadway Books, 1998.

————. *The Miracle of Mindfulness.* Boston: Beacon Press, 1975, 1976.

Hiaasen, Carl. *Sick Puppy.* New York: Alfred A. Knopf, 2000.

Irwin, J., and H. Anisman. "Stress and Pathology: Immunological and Central Nervous System Interactions." In *Psychological Stress and Cancer.* C.L. Cooper (Ed.). New York: John Wiley, 1984.

Jampolsky, Gerald G. *Good-bye to Guilt: Releasing Fear Through Forgiveness.* Toronto: Bantam Books, 1985.

Jensen, Jean C. *Reclaiming Your Life: A Step-by-Step Guide to Using Regression Therapy to Overcome the Effects of Childhood Abuse.* Hammondsworth, Middlesex, England: Dutton, 1995.

Kang, H. S. *Dong Yang Euitiak Gaeron* (Introduction to East Asian Medicine). Seoul: Komun-sa, 1981.

Kohl, MaryAnn and F. Mudwork: *Creative Clay, Dough, and Modeling Experiences.* Bellingham, Wa.: Bright Ring Publishing, 1989.

Kurcinka, Mary Sheedy. *Kids, Parents and Power Struggles: Winning for a Lifetime.* New York: HarperCollins, 2000.

Lee, S. H. *In This Earth and That Wind: This Is Korea.* D. I Steinberg (Trans.). Seoul: Hollym. Corp., 1967.

Lefkowitz, Bernard. *Our Guys.* New York: Random House, Vintage Books, 1997.

Lerner, Harriet, Ph.D. *The Dance of Anger.* New York: HarperPerennial, 1985, 1997.

Lerner, Michael. *Surplus Powerlessness.* Oakland, Calif.: The Institute for Labor and Mental Health, 1986.

Licata, Renora. *Everything You Need to Know About Anger.* New York: The Rosen Publishing Group, 1992, 1994.

Luskin, Fred. *Forgive for Good: A Proven Prescription for Health and Happiness.* San Francisco: Harper San Francisco, 2002.

McKay, Matthew, Davis, Martha, and Fanning, Patrick. *Messages: The Communication Skills Book.* Oakland, Calif.: New Harbinger Publications, 1983.

Middelton-Moz, Jane. *Boiling Point: The High Cost of Unhealthy Anger to Individuals and Society.* Deerfield Beach, Fla.: Health Communications, Inc., 1999.

———. *Boiling Point: The Workbook, Dealing With the Anger in Our Lives.* Deerfield Beach, Fla.: Health Communications, Inc., 2000.

———. *Children of Trauma: Rediscovering Your Discarded Self.* Deerfield Beach, Fla.: Health Communications, Inc., 1989.

———. *Shame and Guilt: Masters of Disguise.* Deerfield Beach, Fla.: Health Communications, Inc., 1990.

———. *Will to Survive: Affirming the Positive Power of the Human Spirit.* Deerfield Beach, Fla.: Health Communications, In., 1992

———. *Welcoming Our Children to a New Millennium: A Daybook of Hopes and Wishes for the Future.* Deerfield Beach, Fla.: Health Communications, Inc., 1999.

Middelton-Moz, Jane, and Lorie Dwinell. *After the Tears: Reclaiming the Personal Losses of Childhood.* Deerfield Beach, Fla.: Health Communications, Inc., 1986.

Middelton-Moz, Jane, and Mary Lee Zawadski. *Bullies: From the Playground to the Boardroom; Strategies for Survival.* Deerfield Beach, Fla.: Health Communications, Inc., 2002.

Miller, Alice. *The Untouched Key: Tracing Childhood Trauma in Creativity and Destructiveness.* New York: Doubleday, 1988.

Millman, Dan, illustrated by Bruce T. Taylor. *Secret of the Peaceful Warrior.* Tiburon, Calif.: Starseed Press, 1991.

Novotni, Michele and Petersen, Randy. *Angry with God.* Colorado Springs, Colo.: Pinon Press, 2001.

Pennebaker, James W. *Opening Up: The Healing Power of Expressing Emotions.* New York: The Guilford Press, 1990.

Pliskin, Rabbi Zelig. *Anger! The Inner Teacher.* New York: Mesorah Publications, Ltd. 1997.

Pollack, William S. *Real Boys' Voices.* New York: Penguin Books, 2000.

Porro, Barbara. Illustrations by Peaco Todd. *Talk It Out: Conflict Resolution in the Elementary Classroom.* Alexandria, Va.: ASCD, 1996.

———. *Teaching Conflict Resolution with the Rainbow Kids Program.* Illustrations by Peaco Todd. Alexandria, Va.: ASCD, 2002.

Rinpoche, Soygal. *The Tibetan Book of Living and Dying.* San Francisco: Harper San Francisco, 2002.

Rosenberg, Marhsall B. *Nonviolent Communication: A Language of Compassion.* Encinitas, Calif.: PuddleDancer Press, 1999.

Rubin, Theodore, I. *Compassion and Self-Hate: An Alternative to Despair.* New York: Simon & Schuster, Touchstone Books, 1975.

Schiraldi, Glenn R., Ph.D., and Melissa Hallmark Kerr, Ph.D. *The Anger Management Sourcebook.* Chicago: Contemporary Books, 2002.

Seligman, Martin E. P. *Helplessness: On Depression, Development, and Death.* New York: W.H. Freeman and Company, 1975.

Smedes, Lewis B. *The Art of Forgiving: When You Need to Forgive and Don't Know How.* New York: Ballantine Books, 1996.

Tavris, Carol. *Anger: The Misunderstood Emotion.* New York: Simon & Schuster, 1982, 1989.

Todd, Peaco. *The Girl's Guide to Football.* N. Cambridge, Mass.: Cactus Studio Press, 2000.

Valentis, Mary, Ph.D., and Anne Devane, Ph.D. *Female Rage: Unlocking Its Secrets, Claiming Its Power.* New York: Carol Southern Books, 1994.

Warren, Neil Clark. *Make Anger Your Ally.* Colorado Springs, Colo.: Focus on the Family Publishing, 1990.

Worthington, Everett. *Five Steps to Forgiveness: The Art and Science of Forgiving.* New York: Crown Publishers, 2001.

Periodicals

Atkinson, Brent, "Brain to Brain." *Psychotherapy Networker,* September/October 2002.

The Brown University Child and Adolescent Behavior Letter. July 1999, 15, 7.

Chikly, Alaya, "Heart Centered Therapy: Assume Only Love." *Massage Today,* November 2002, 2, 11.

Deffenbacher, Jerry L., Eugene R. Oetting and Raymond A. DiGiuseppe, "Principles of Empirically Supported Interventions Applied to Anger Management." *The Counseling Psychologist,* 30, 2, March 2002.

Farthing, Michael J. G., "Irritable Bowel, Irritable Body, or Irritable Brain?" *British Medical Journal.* January 21, 1995, 310, 6973.

Fox, B. H. "The Role of Psychological Factors in Cancer Incidence and Prognosis." *Oncology* 9/3 (1995).

Kaplan, S., L. A. Go, H. S. Chalk, E. Magliocco, D. Rohouit, and W. Ross. "Hostility in Verbal Productions and Hypnotic Dreams in Hypertensive Patients." *Psychosomatic Medicine* 23 (1961).

Lipton, Bruce H., PhD. "Insight Into Cellular 'Consciousness.'" *Bridges,* 12 (2001) (1):5

———. "The Biology of Belief." *www.spiritcrossing.com / lipton / biology.shtm* (2001)

Mann, A. H. "Psychiatric Morbidity and Hostility in Hypertension," *Psychological Medicine* 7 (1977).

Pang, Keum Young. "Hwabyung: The Construction of a Korean Popular Illness Among Korean Elderly Immigrant Women in the United States." *Culture, Medicine and Psychiatry* 144 (December 1990).

Wylie, Mary Sykes and Richard Simon, "Discoveries from the Black Box." *Psychotherapy Networker,* September/October 2002.

Other Resources

Alcoholics Anonymous; (212) 870-3400; *www.alcoholics-anonymous.org.*

Childhelp USA. If you need help or suspect abuse call the CHILDHELP USA® NATIONAL CHILD ABUSE HOTLINE: 1-800-4-ACHILD®, 24 hours a day.

Emotional literacy for children: Crary, Elizabeth and Peaco Todd. *Feeling Elf Cards and Games.* Seattle: Parenting Press, 2002.

HeartMath® Institute offers a wealth of information on managing anger. You can learn more about the HeartMath on their Web site: *www.heartmath.com.*

Lipton, Bruce H., Ph.D. *The Biology of Belief* videotape. For more information and to order: *www.brucelipton.com.*

Multiple Chemical Sensitivities: MCS Referral and Resources, *www.mcsrr.org*; (410) 362-6400.

Narcotics Anonymous; (818) 773-9999; *www.na.org.*

National Child Abuse Hotline: Child Help USA: (800) 422-4453. You can call this number if you feel that you're in danger of abusing your child.

PMS: National Association for Premenstrual Syndrome (UK); *www.pms.org.uk.*

Sugar Habit: Overeaters Anonymous, (505) 891-2664; *www.overeatersanonymous.org.*

ABOUT THE AUTHORS

Jane Middelton-Moz, M.S., is a trainer, consultant and community interventionist. She speaks internationally on issues of multigenerational grief and trauma, anger, bullies and bullying, and cultural and ethnic self-hate. She has appeared on national radio and television, including: *Oprah, Montel, Maury Povich* and PBS. She is the author of *Children of Trauma; Shame and Guilt; Boiling Point; Boiling Point: The Workbook; Welcoming Our Children to the New Millennium;* and coauthor of *After the Tears* and *Bullies: From the Playground to the Boardroom.* The Web site for the Middelton-Moz Institute is *www.ippi.org.*

Lisa Tener, M.S., has led workshops and seminars since 1994. Her television appearances include *ABC World News with Peter Jennings* and WCVB's *Chronicle.* She has been interviewed and quoted in magazines and newspapers, including *Family Circle,* the *Boston Globe* and *Hope.* Her studies and interest in alternative healing modalities led her to develop the concept of *Anger-obics*^{SM}, a holistic approach to anger, which emphasizes exercises that employ creativity, humor and a person's inner wisdom. She received her bachelor's and master's degrees from MIT.

Peaco Todd, M.A., is a syndicated cartoonist and writer whose book and illustration credits include: *Talk It Out; The Rainbow Kids Program; Frame by Frame; The Girl's Guide to Football; Family Matters* and the *Feeling Elf* cards. A national speaker on cartoons as communications strategy since 1991, she also has been a commentator on NPR and is a faculty member in Lesley University's Learning Community Bachelor's program. Her Web site is *www.peacotoons.com.*

Also by Jane Middelton-Moz

By encouraging awareness and accountability *Boiling Point* and *Boiling Point: The Workbook* show you how to develop the ability to express anger in healthy ways for optimum personal growth.

Code #6676 • $10.95

Code #7567 • $12.95

In *Bullies*, the authors present interviews with the bullies and with the people they've abused; strategies to cope with (and avoid altogether) bullying situations; and analysis of playground, relationship and workspace bullies.

Code #9861 • $12.95

More from the Author

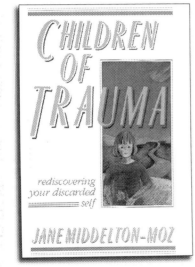

This book describes how debilitating shame and guilt are created and fostered in childhood and how they manifest themselves in adulthood and intimate relationships.

Code #0147 • $9.95

Unresolved childhood trauma can reverberate through generations. This insightful masterpiece takes you by the hand and leads you on a journey toward self-love and self acceptance.

Code #0724 • $8.95

Your Starting Place for Inspiration

Daily Affirmations For Forgiving & Moving On offers you hope, strength and inspiration.

Code #2158 • Paperback •$7.95

Dayton's companion to her best-selling recovery classic *Daily Affirmations For Forgiving & Moving On* is beautifully written and will open your eyes to the liberating power of forgiveness.

Code #0863 • Paperback • $12.95